GreenSmoothieGirl.com
Readers' Favorite
Healthy Recipes

55% All Raw, 85% Vegan, & 90% Gluten Free

~ Volume 2 ~

by
Robyn Openshaw

GreenSmoothieGirl.com Readers' Favorite Healthy Recipes, Volume 2

Published by Robyn Openshaw/GreenSmoothieGirl.com
Lindon, UT
December 2011

ISBN 978-0-9831113-9-9

Printed in the United States of America.

Disclaimer

Nothing in this book is intended to claim to diagnose, treat, cure, or prevent any disease. This book is not a substitute for primary medical care, but should be seen rather as an educational resource.

Trademarks

All trademarks mentioned are the property of their respective owners.

Contents

(R=Raw recipe, V=Vegan recipe, GF=Gluten-free recipe)

Main Dishes

Side Dishes

Chili, Soups, Stews, & Sandwiches

Chili

Soups

Salads & Dressings

Desserts

Pies, Cakes, & Frostings

Frozen Treats

Puddings & Custards

Other Desserts

About the Author

Robyn Openshaw grew up the eldest of eight children, raised on a tight budget where the menu was dominated by simple plant foods: whole grains and legumes, greens, fruits and vegetables, and nuts and seeds.

She has a Web site, GreenSmoothieGirl.com, with tens of thousands of new visitors monthly, dedicated to helping people achieve high energy and vibrant health. Its mission is to teach families how to live a whole-food lifestyle (mostly plants and 60-80% raw) diet that is easy, inexpensive, and delicious—in addition to nourishing.

Robyn taught at a university and now lectures all over the U.S. She is the author of the *12 Steps to Whole Foods* course, *The Green Smoothies Diet*, and several recipe books. She is also the author of two children's books, *The Adventures of Junk Food Dude* and *Junk Food Dude's Yummy Healthy Recipes*.

She is a single mom of four competitive athletes with high-caloric needs who help develop and test her recipes. She received undergraduate and graduate degrees from BYU and the University of Utah and loves "arranging the elements" in the kitchen, reading and writing, cycling, running, skiing, and competitive tennis.

Acknowledgments

Recipe categorization: Desirée Ward

Desirée reviewed the readers' recipes to determine if they qualified as being raw, vegan, and/or gluten free. She also occasionally suggested ingredient substitutions in order to make a recipe fit into one or more of the three categories. Her Web site featuring whole-food and gluten-free cooking is www.unconventionalkitchen.com. Contact her at desiree@unconventionalkitchen.com.

Food staging & photography: Katie Dudley

Katie is a genius with food photography, which isn't an easy subject. I know tons of photographers but recruited her specifically to shoot my recipes. Contact her at katiedudley3@gmail.com.

Editing & page design: Deb Tokarewich

Deb is a language master par excellence and nonpareil, with a fine eye for detail. (I'm a former editor and know good from better from best; thus I hire only the finest.) She also loves playing with templates, fonts, graphics, and other page design stuff. Contact her at dtokarewich@yahoo.com.

Cover design: Alana Mae Jenkins

Alana Mae's cover beat 169 other designs in a contest because I fell madly in love with her creation—it's feminine and fanciful, artistic and attention grabbing. Contact her at southcoastdesigner@hotmail.com.

Introduction

Before I radically changed my diet and thereby transformed my family's health, my best and most used recipe books were the "Favorites" collections. The business school of the university where I taught, the church congregation of my childhood, my mother-in-law's church congregation, even the U.S. Congress (whose recipe book I received in Washington D.C. when I got married)…they all put together their community's best recipes.

I always figured that something others use a few times a month, which might be loved for generations in a family, is worth a try.

The problem is, when you submit your favorite recipes, you want everyone to be impressed by how the recipe tastes. In America, that means lots of refined foods: sugar, white flour, toxic salt and, oh, a nearly endless litany of fatty ingredients.

One "favorite" in my religious community is called Funeral Potatoes because we always serve it after funerals. (It may be actually contributing to more funerals.) It contains sour cream, cheddar cheese, cream of chicken soup (with monosodium glutamate), greasy hash browns, and margarine.

Three years after putting GreenSmoothieGirl.com up, I had the largest community of whole-foods enthusiasts on the Internet—and maybe in the world. Tens of thousands read my newsletter and blog and follow my 12 Steps to Whole Foods program. One day I thought to myself, why not gather the best *healthy* recipes of my readers and put the collection out there?

And that's what this is. It's the only Favorites collection that I know of that focuses on high nutrition!

I confess I've combed through the recipes and made substitutions. If you said salt, I substituted sea (unrefined) salt. If you said sugar, I changed it to raw coconut sugar or Sucanat. If you said dairy or soy milk, I replaced it with rice or almond milk. If you said flour, I said whole-grain flour. Stuff like that. If an ingredient didn't qualify as a whole food, I made my standard substitutions.

I also confess that I haven't tested all the recipes like I do when I develop my own. I've trusted my readers. So, a caveat: you'll have to trust each other.

Keep in mind that some of my readers are long-time raw foodists, so some recipes are all raw. And some readers are new to the whole-foods journey, so their recipes may not qualify under your personal nutrition standards.

You'll get a somewhat wide variety of what's considered "healthy." But these are the recipes that make you love being health minded—recipes that taste good but also nourish you.

Thank you to all my amazing readers who contributed recipes! Each recipe has an attribution line directly beneath its title. The recipes are organized alphabetically in each section according to the contributors' first names (*not* by the recipe names). Names are written same as they were submitted; occasionally a contributor's website or blog is also included. And if I "tweaked" a recipe a bit to use even more healthful ingredients, there's an additional attribution line noting that. Last but not least, there is a letter designation after a recipe name if it qualifies as being an all-raw (R), vegan (V), and/or gluten-free (GF) recipe.

There are photos of some of the recipes in a section near the middle of the book. Each is captioned with the recipe title and page number where the recipe can be found. Recipes that have photos in this section have a "[See Photos section.]" reference at the end of the recipe. (Note that these references as well as the photo captions are hot links in the PDF version of the book; clicking on them will take you directly from the recipe to its photo, and vice versa.)

I hope you find lots of new favorites for your own arsenal. That's the key to vibrant nutrition and optimal health: having a repertoire of great recipes so you look forward to your nutritious meals and snacks.

Enjoy!

~ *Robyn Openshaw*

Main Dishes

Main Dishes

Spaghetti Squash Lasagna (GF)

Thanks for the recipe, Alicia!

> 1 large spaghetti squash
> vegetables of your choice, chopped (onion, carrots, zucchini, bell peppers, spinach, etc.)
> extra virgin olive oil (enough to sauté veggies)
> 2 cans crushed tomatoes
> 3-5 garlic cloves, minced
> 1 tsp. basil
> ½ tsp. oregano
> 1 C grated mozzarella cheese
> ½ C grated Parmesan cheese

Preheat oven to 375°. Bake the spaghetti squash and shred to create "noodles." Sauté the vegetables, then add the tomatoes, garlic, basil, and oregano to them and mix all together well. Then add "noodles" to veggie mixture and toss together. Put half the veggie/ "noodle" mixture in a 9"x13" pan and sprinkle half the cheeses on top. Then repeat the layers, using the other half of the ingredients. Bake for 30 min. Let cool 15 min. before serving.

Quinoa and Beans and Salsa (V,GF)

Thanks for the recipe, Alicia Royer!

This is a wonderful slow cooker recipe.

> 2 (16 oz.) cans black beans, drained and rinsed
> 1 (14 oz.) can vegetable broth
> 1 C uncooked quinoa
> 1 qt. salsa (preferably homemade)
> 1 C water
> ½ tsp. garlic powder

Combine all ingredients into slow cooker and stir well. Cover and cook on low 8-10 hrs. (If you have a slow cooker like mine, it will cook in 2- 4 hrs., so watch it!) [See Photos section.]

Pass the Mac and Cheese Please (GF)

Thanks for the recipe, Anna Romano (www.annadote.com)!

16 oz. brown rice penne pasta
24 oz. low-fat cottage cheese
⅓ C grated Parmesan cheese
2 C grated raw goat cheddar cheese (or any white cheddar), divided
1 Tbsp. ghee (clarified butter)

Preheat oven to 375°. Boil pasta according to package directions. Drain, then add ghee, cottage cheese, parmesan cheese, and 1 C cheddar cheese. Mix well, then pour into a 2 qt. casserole dish and sprinkle the remaining 1 C cheddar cheese (and extra Parmesan, if desired) on top. Bake for 35 min. Serve with lots of greens and enjoy! [See Photos section.]

Kale and Black Bean Tacos (V,GF)

Thanks for the recipe, April (www.health4lifecooking.blogspot.com)!

1 garlic clove, minced
1 C water + 1 Tbsp. Bragg Liquid Aminos or tamari (to make a broth) [Use tamari for GF recipe.]
1 large bunch kale, finely chopped
1 Tbsp. Mrs. Dash Southwest Chipotle *OR* 2 tsp. chili powder + 1 tsp. ground cumin + 1 tsp. coriander
2 C cooked black beans
½ large (or 1 small) avocado, mashed

Add garlic, broth, and kale to a medium sauce pan. Cover, bring to boil, lower heat to medium, and cook 5 min. until bright green. Reduce to a simmer, add seasonings, and continue cooking for 10 min. or until kale is very tender. Add black beans and cook an additional 5 min. Remove from heat and add mashed avocado. Soften corn tortillas on a dry skillet and fill with mixture. *Makes 8-10 tacos.*

Lentil-Rice Balls (V)

Thanks for the recipe, Brynna!

½ C brown rice, rinsed and drained
½ C lentils, rinsed and drained (any color but red)
½ C whole-wheat flour
¾ tsp. aluminum-free baking powder
½ tsp. sea salt
1 tsp. Italian seasoning
¼ tsp. garlic powder
1 tsp. cumin
freshly ground pepper, to taste

Place the rice and lentils in a small saucepan and add 2 C water. Bring to a boil, lower the heat, and cover with a lid. Cook on low for 30-40 min., until soft. Remove from heat and drain the rice and lentils thoroughly in a fine-mesh sieve to remove any excess water.

Preheat the oven to 350°. Line a baking sheet with parchment paper, spray with nonstick spray, and set aside.

When the rice and lentils are cool enough to touch, process in the food processor until semi-smooth. Then place mixture in a bowl, add the remaining ingredients, and mix well with your hands. Press mixture into meatball shapes, about the size of walnuts. Place balls on the baking sheet. (At this point, you can refrigerate them until ready to bake.)

Brush a tiny bit of olive oil on top of each ball (is fine without oil also) and bake until browned and crispy on the outside, about 30-35 min., turning once halfway through baking.

Use these anywhere you use meatballs—soups, subs, pasta, etc. So, so good! My kids will eat the leftovers cold out of the fridge! *Makes 24 balls.*

Veggie Balls or Burgers (V,GF)

Thanks for the recipe, Christopher O Baum!

> 2 C cooked short-grain brown rice
>
> ½ C ground raw almonds
>
> 2 Tbsp. arrowroot powder or whole-grain flour
>
> 2-3 Tbsp. extra virgin olive oil
>
> 1 C chopped onion
>
> 1 C small-chopped broccoli
>
> 1 C small-chopped carrots
>
> 1½ C small-chopped mushrooms
>
> 1 C small-chopped celery
>
> ½ C chopped black olives
>
> 2 cloves garlic, minced
>
> 2 cubes Better Than Bouillon [If use a different bouillon, make sure it's gluten free for a GF recipe.]
>
> 2-3 tsp. tamari sauce
>
> 3-4 tsp. dried parsley *OR* 2-3 Tbsp. chopped fresh
>
> 1 tsp. dill weed
>
> 1 tsp. paprika
>
> ½ tsp. marjoram
>
> ½ tsp. thyme
>
> *optional*: ½ C walnuts, chopped

Preheat oven to 400°. Mix first three ingredients together and set aside.

Heat the oil and sauté the onions, broccoli, and carrots until semi tender. Add the other vegetables and sauté 1-2 min. Add the other vegetables and sauté 1-2 min. more. Add all the remaining ingredients and sauté another 1-2 min. Break up bouillon and add to stir fry and mix well.

Remove sauté from heat and mix it well with the rice mixture. Roll into balls using ⅛ - ¼ C for each and bake for 18-22 min.

To make burger patties, use ½ - ¾ C mixture for each and lightly coat patty with whole-wheat, spelt, or kamut flour. Grill or lightly fry in pan for 4-5 min. on each side. Serve with favorite burger toppings on a bun. Enjoy!

Best Raw Burgers Ever (R,V,GF)

Thanks for the recipe, Corrine!

> 1 C pecans or walnuts
> 1 C sweet onion
> 1 C mushrooms
> 1 tsp. cumin
> 2 tsp. chili powder
> 2 tsp. Arizona Chipotle (available at www.Anthonyspices.com)
> 1-2 Tbsp. water, as needed

Process all ingredients in food processor until you reach the desired consistency for your burgers. Shape into patties and dehydrate for 2 hrs., then flip and dehydrate 4 hrs. more. Do not over-dehydrate; leave burgers a little moist in the middle.

I like to cut two slices of tomatoes and put a burger patty, ketchup, lettuce, and avocado on top of one slice and then top it with the other slice of tomato and eat it like a sandwich. [See Photos section.]

Salsa Pizza (GF)

Thanks for the recipe, Deana!

(Recipe was adapted by Robyn.)

> 1 handful cilantro
> 10-12 Roma tomatoes
> 1 small (or ½ large) yellow onion
> 2 garlic cloves
> 1 jalapeño pepper
> juice of ½ lime
> juice of ½ lemon
> ½ bag corn (run warm water over it to thaw it out)
> 1 red bell pepper, diced
> sprouted tortillas [Use corn tortillas for GF recipe.]
> shredded cheese (low-fat or no-fat)

In blender or processor, pulse the first seven ingredients a few times to mix well and get the salsa texture. Add the salsa to a large bowl and mix in the corn and bell pepper.

Turn broiler on so you can crisp the tortillas. Then turn on the oven and on the crisped tortillas, first sprinkle some cheese and then top with the salsa. Heat just until the cheese melts and the salsa is warmed. [See Photos section.]

Quick-and-Easy Veggie Burgers (V,GF)

Thanks for the recipe, Desirée Hancock (www.unconventionalkitchen.com)!

Make sure to mash your beans really well so that the patties hold together. I sometimes blend my beans before so that they stick together nicely.

> 1 C chopped onion
> ½ C chopped sweet peppers
> 4 garlic cloves
> 2 tsp. extra virgin olive oil
> ½ C peeled and grated carrots
> 3 tsp. chili powder
> 2 tsp. cumin
> 3 C cooked black beans
> 3 Tbsp. dijon mustard
> 3 Tbsp. soy sauce
> 3 Tbsp. ketchup or tomato paste
> Tobasco, to taste
> 1½ C rolled oats (don't substitute instant oats)

Sauté the onions, sweet peppers, and garlic in the oil for about 5 min., until the onions begin to soften. Add the carrots, chili powder, and cumin, and cook on low heat for 5 min. Set aside.

Mash the beans in a large bowl with a potato masher or the back of a spoon. Add the mustard, soy sauce, ketchup/tomato paste, and the sauteed vegetable. Form into patties. Fry them in a fry pan until warmed through and slightly crisp on the oustide. Cast iron frying pans make the best veggie burgers.

The Whole Enchilada with Caramelized Onions (V,GF)

Thanks for the recipe, Desirée Hancock (www.unconventionalkitchen.com)!

These enchiladas freeze well. You can either cook them and then freeze them in smaller portions or freeze them uncooked and then bake them after they are mostly thawed in a 350° oven until heated through. I recommend making these in layers like a lasagna if you are going to freeze them.

> *Tip:* To help your corn tortillas keep from baking, warm them in a frying pan before rolling them, then quickly transfer them to a baking dish that has sauce in the bottom of it to fill and roll them.

corn tortillas (10-12)

2½ C chopped sweet potato

1 can (15 oz.) black beans

1 can (4 oz.) fire-roasted chilis

1 tsp. cumin

1 tsp. coriander

¼ C cilantro, chopped

2 limes

salt and pepper, to taste

1 large jar tomatillo salsa (good quality; check for real ingredients)

optional: sharp cheddar cheese [Omit for V recipe.]

Preheat oven to 350°. Peel and chop the sweet potatoes into small pieces. Bring a medium-sized pot of water to a boil, then add the sweet potatoes. While potatoes are cooking, start caramelizing the onions (recipe below). Cook the potatoes until fork tender.

Drain the water from the sweet potatoes, then pour them into a bowl and add the black beans, cumin, coriander, cilantro, roasted chilies, and salt and pepper. Put the tortillas in the oven while it is heating up to get them soft. Pull them out a few at a time and fill each with the sweet potato mixture and a few caramelized onions, then roll up to close. Place the tortillas seam-side down in a 9"x13" glass pan. Continue to fill all of the tortillas until the mixture is gone. Pour the salsa over the enchiladas, then top them with the cheese.

Cover the pan with foil and bake for 15 min. Remove the foil and bake 10 min. more. If you want a crunchy top, broil them at the end for a couple of minutes. Garnish with salsa, guacamole, and fresh cilantro. *Makes 6 servings*.

Caramelized Onions:

1 tsp. extra virgin olive oil

1 tsp. butter or another 1 tsp. of olive oil

1 medium/large onion

½ tsp. Sucanat

Melt butter and olive oil in a large frying pan, then add the onion. Cook until soft, then add the Sucanat. Continue to cook 20 min. until brown and caramelized.

Leek Lentils (V)

Thanks for the recipe, Evi from Germany!

(Recipe was adapted by Robyn.)

> 2 large leeks
> 1 C vegetable broth
> ⅔ C dry red lentils, washed
> 1 Tbsp. extra virgin olive oil
> 5 Tbsp. heavy cream of choice (oat cream, etc.) [Use oat cream for V recipe.]
> 2 tsp. mustard (spicy/hot)
> 1 handful Italian (flat-leaf) parsley, chopped
> sea salt and pepper, to taste
> splash of lemon juice
> bit of sweetener (Sucanat, raw agave/honey) [Use agave or Sucanat for V recipe.]

Wash and dry the leeks. Cut then into fine rings and sauté in the olive oil. Add broth, cover, and cook for 5 min.

Add lentils to the leeks and heat for 2-3 min. Then add the cream and mustard, bring to a boil, reduce heat, and cook an additional 2-3 min. Season to taste with pepper, salt, lemon juice, and a wee bit of sweetener. Sprinkle with chopped parsley.

Please note the lentils are not cooked to utter softness as usual, but I liked that. Eat as a meal on its own or mix with brown rice, quinoa, whole grain spaghetti, etc. Can also be served as a side dish.

Portobello Burgers (V,GF)

Thanks for the recipe, Evi from Germany!

> 4 large Portobello mushrooms, stems removed
>
> 1 Tbsp. extra virgin olive oil
>
> ⅔ C water
>
> sea salt and ground pepper, to taste
>
> 1 ripe avocado, pitted, peeled, and roughly chopped
>
> 1 Tbsp. spicy brown mustard
>
> 1 Tbsp. horseradish
>
> 1 Tbsp. fresh lime juice
>
> 4 whole-grain hamburger rolls, split horizontally [Use gluten-free buns for GF recipe.]
>
> 4 thin slices beefsteak tomato
>
> *optional*: 1 jalapeño chili pepper (ribs and seeds removed, if you want less heat), finely chopped

Preheat oven to 425°. On a large, rimmed baking sheet, toss mushrooms with oil and water, then season with salt and pepper. Arrange stemmed-side down and cover loosely with foil. Roast until tender, 30-45 min. Meanwhile, in a medium mixing bowl, mash avocado with a fork, then stir in mustard, horseradish, and lime juice. Fold in optional jalapeño, then season with salt and pepper. Toast the rolls. To assemble, on bottom half of each roll, layer a tomato slice, a Portobello, and the avocado mixture. Cap off with top half of roll and enjoy! *Makes 4 burgers.*

Vegetable Lasagna (V)

Thanks for the recipe, Evi from Germany!

½ C raw almonds

½ C raw walnuts

1 onion, thinly sliced

2 garlic cloves, minced

1 C fresh basil leaves

1/8 tsp. nutmeg

1/8 tsp. sea salt

black pepper, to taste

½ C water

1 C organic marinara sauce (or homemade sauce)

4 oz. uncooked whole-wheat lasagne noodles

2 C spinach, well washed

2 C fresh tomatoes, sliced and chopped *OR* canned no-salt-added diced
   tomatoes

Preheat oven to 375°. Coat a 9" square pan with cooking spray or canola oil. Combine the almonds, walnuts, onion, garlic, basil, nutmeg, salt, pepper, and water in a food processor until smooth, about 1 min. Spread ½ C of the marinara sauce on the bottom of the pan. Cover with pieces of uncooked noodles, 1 C spinach, 1 C tomatoes, and half of the nut mixture. Repeat the layers again. Bake for 50 min., until lightly browned. *Makes 4 servings.*

Yummy Vegan Burgers with Pesto and Salsa (V)

Thanks for the recipe, Evi from Germany!

2 C oatmeal, uncooked

1 C sunflower seeds

¼ C dried mushroom pieces, ground (shiitake or your choice)

½ C spelt or whole-grain flour

1 Tbsp. fennel seeds

¼ C nutritional yeast

¼ C dried parsley flakes

¼ C sesame seeds

¼ C wheat germ

2 C grated carrot

1 onion, finely chopped

2 garlic cloves, minced

¼ C Bragg Liquid Aminos

2 C water

whole-grain burger buns (~ 12)

pesto (homemade or store bought)

salsa (homemade or store bought)

veggie mayonnaise

Preheat oven to 375°. Using a food processor, mix oatmeal, sunflower seeds, and mushrooms until grainy in consistency and sunflower seeds are very finely chopped. Transfer mixture to a large mixing bowl and add next five ingredients. Mix and form a well for wet ingredients.

In a separate bowl, combine next six ingredients and mix well. Then add to dry ingredients and mix very well with a large spoon. With oiled hands, scoop a heaping tablespoon onto the palm of your hand and form into a ball (3" in diameter). Place onto a cookie sheet with baking paper on it and flatten to about ½" in thickness. Bake for 10-12 min. Turn patties and bake for an additional 10-12 min.

Toast buns and spread with veggie mayonnaise and pesto. Place hot patties on buns and top with salsa. Serve with a salad on the side. *Makes approximately 12 burgers.*

Tip: These burger patties freeze well and can be easily reheated in the oven or a microwave. You could also top them with vegan gravy and serve with potatoes or brown rice for a hearty supper.

Brown Rice & Quinoa Sushi Rolls (V,GF)

Thanks for the recipe, Genevieve!

⅔ C short-grain brown rice
2⅓ C water
dash sea salt
½ C quinoa
2 Tbsp. rice vinegar
1 Tbsp. raw apple cider vinegar *OR* 3 Tbsp. rice vinegar
2 Tbsp. coconut palm sugar or Sucanat
½ tsp. sea salt
4 nori sheets
½ carrot, grated
½ cucumber, cut into thin strips
1 avocado, cut into strips (about ¼" square)
optional: 1 Tbsp. mirin
optional: dash sesame seeds (or try Eden Food's Gomasio)
optional: 2 Tbsp. Vegannaise (mixed with a little wasabi)
optional: wasabi, pickled ginger, and tamari or Nama Shoyu (for serving)

Rinse and drain the rice, then add it to a medium size saucepan along with the salt and water. (That's too much water for the rice, but you'll add the quinoa to it as well later on). Bring to a boil, reduce heat to low, and cover the pan. Set a timer for 30 min.

While the rice cooks, mix up the vinegars, sugar, salt, and optional mirin. I like to heat this up so that the sugar and salt fully dissolve. Set aside. Also while the rice cooks, you can grate the carrot, slice the cucumber, and cut up the avocado, and then set aside.

At the 30-min. mark, add in the quinoa to the rice pan and give it a quick stir. You may have to bring it back up to a boil to maintain the heat, then reduce it back down to low and cover again. Set the timer for 15 more min., after which the rice and the quinoa should be tender and nicely cooked.

Remove the rice mixture from the pan and turn it into a large mixing bowl, or even onto a cookie sheet so that it cools more quickly. Mix in the vinegar mixture, carefully folding it into the rice. I like to use a rice paddle (flat sort of spoon), fanning it out as I go to help the rice cool off. Adjust the seasoning if need be, adding more vinegar if you like. (I wouldn't add more salt because you generally serve with soy sauce.)

After about 10 min., the rice should have cooled off quite a bit and be ready to work with. (You could prepare this far in advance, remembering it's best to work with the rice at room temperature.)

Cover up a sushi mat with plastic wrap or a clear plastic bag (I put it inside a large Ziploc bag). Place a sheet of nori on your mat, shiny side down. Eyeball your rice mixture into four equal portions and place one portion on the nori sheet. Pat it down with damp hands to cover the lower half of the nori sheet with rice. (There is usually a picture on the back of the nori packaging to show you how to spread the rice and roll it up. I like to keep a mug of water nearby to dip my fingers into.)

If you like, spread a thin layer of mayo across the rice, with the additional option of adding a little wasabi to the mayo. Another option is to sprinkle the rice with sesame seeds or Gomasio at this point. Place your fillings in a straight line across the middle of your rice. Lift the sushi mat and fold over and roll, forming a log. This might take practice if it's your first time, but basically connect the bottom of the sheet closest to you to the top of the rice mixture, which should result in your filling being perfectly in the middle (or not—but still tastes good!). Use the mat to help you tighten up the sushi log, then release it.

Repeat to use up all the rice and you should have four sushi logs. With a very sharp knife (I like to use a bread knife), cut each log into six or eight equal pieces. Serve with wasabi, picked ginger and light soy sauce. Enjoy! *Makes enough to fill 4 nori sheets, which you can cut into 6 or 8 pieces each.*

Polenta with Caramelized Onions & Roasted Red Peppers (GF)

Thanks for the recipe, Janelle!

> 1 C uncooked polenta
> 3 C water
> 1 Tbsp. butter
> ½ tsp. sea salt (or to taste)
> ¼ C Parmesan cheese
> 2 red peppers
> 2 Tbsp. coconut oil
> 1 onion, sliced very thin (with a mandolin if possible)
> ½ C shredded sharp cheddar cheese

Boil polenta in water for 5 min. Remove from heat and stir in butter, Parmesan cheese, and salt. Pour into a 7"x11" pan and let sit until firm.

Meanwhile, turn on broiler. Put the pepper on a piece of parchment paper in a jelly roll pan and place it under the broiler 4-6 in. from heat. Watch it carefully and turn it as it starts to blacken. When the pepper is blackened on all sides, remove it from the oven, place it inside a Ziploc bag lined with parchment paper (you will not be able to use your bag again!), and let it cool.

Preheat the oven to 350°. When the pepper is cooled, peel the skin off, remove the seeds, and dice it. To caramelize the onion, melt the coconut oil in a skillet (preferably *not* non-stick, like a cast-iron skillet). Add the onion slices and stir until they begin to brown, then remove from heat.

Evenly spread the onions on top of the polenta, then layer with diced roasted peppers, and top with cheese. Bake until the cheese melts. *Serves 3 as a main dish, 6 as a side dish.*

Lentil Tacos (V,GF)

Thanks for the recipe, Jennifer!

> 1 Tbsp. extra virgin olive oil
> 1 C finely chopped onion
> 1 garlic clove
> ½ tsp. sea salt
> 1 C brown lentils, rinsed
> 1 pkg. taco seasoning (or make your own!)
> 2½ C vegetable broth [Use gluten-free broth for GF recipe.]
> 4 taco shells or whole-wheat tortillas [Use corn shells or tortillas for GF recipe.]
> toppings you like (shredded lettuce, tomatoes, avocado, olives, etc.)

Heat oil in skillet over medium-high heat. Cook the onion, garlic, and salt until onion is soft. Add the lentils and taco seasoning and cook until the lentils dry out a bit (a few minutes). Then add the broth and bring to a boil. Reduce the heat and simmer until lentils are tender (½ hr. or so). Uncover and cook some more until they thicken a bit, and then mash them a bit, leaving some whole. Fill taco shells/tortillas and garnish with toppings (I avoid cheese and sour cream and don't miss them at all!). *Serves 4.* [See Photos section.]

Luscious Lentils (V,GF)

Thanks for the recipe, Jennifer!

> 12 oz. brown lentils, rinsed
> 4⅓ C water, divided
> few garlic cloves, minced
> 1 onion, chopped
> 3-4 green onions (scallions), chopped
> 2 celery stalks, chopped
> ¼ C Nama Shoyu or Bragg Liquid Aminos [Use Bragg for GF recipe.]
> ⅓ C balsamic vinegar
> 1 (6 oz.) can tomato paste
> 2 tsp. Dijon or yellow mustard
> freshly ground pepper, to taste

Place the lentils in a large pot and cover with 4 C water. Bring to a boil, cover, reduce the heat, and simmer for 1 hour. Sauté the garlic, onion, scallions, and celery in ⅓ C water until soft. Add to the cooked lentils along with the soy sauce, vinegar, tomato paste, mustard, and pepper. Continue to simmer for 1 hour more, covered for a soup-like consistency or uncovered for a thicker consistency.

This can be served over mashed potatoes, brown rice, or toast. I like to double the recipe (since it takes over 2 hrs.) and freeze some for another time. *Serves 4-6.*

Burritos with Quinoa and Jalapeño with Homemade Corn Tortillas (V)

Thanks for the recipe, Jo!

Corn Tortillas:

> 1 C whole-wheat flour
> ½ C corn meal
> dash salt
> 1 egg (organic and free range)
> 1½ C water

Mix all ingredients together. Pour 2-3 spoonfuls onto hot, nonstick griddle and spread out into 6"-8" rounds. Brown on both sides. Set aside.

Filling:

> 2 tsp. extra virgin olive oil
> 1 medium onion, chopped
> 1 garlic clove, chopped
> ½ tsp. chili flakes
> pinch cayenne pepper
> ½ tsp. turmeric
> ½ tsp. cumin
> ½ tsp. sea salt
> 1 jalapeño, seeded, cored, and finely minced
> ¾ C uncooked quinoa, simmered 10 mins. in 1½ C water)
> ¼ C cooked chickpeas, mashed lightly
> chopped cilantro, to taste
> *optional*: salsa and optional sour cream or yogurt (for serving) [Omit sour cream/yogurt for V recipe.]
> *optional*: ½ C grated mozzarella cheese (for filling) [Omit for V recipe.]

Heat the oil in a large pan on medium heat. Add the onion, garlic, chili flakes, spices, and jalapeño pepper. Sauté until the onion is soft, about 5 min. Add the quinoa and chickpeas and continue to sauté until heated through, about 4 min. Make burritos filling the tortillas with quinoa mixture, cilantro, and optional cheese, then top with optional salsa and sour cream/yogurt. *Makes 4 burritos.*

Black Bean Casserole (V)

Thanks for the recipe, Kari!

> 1 medium white or yellow onion, chopped
> 2 (15-oz.) cans diced stewed tomatoes
> 1 C salsa
> 2 (15-oz.) cans black beans, rinsed and drained
> whole-wheat tortillas
> *optional*: shredded Monterey Jack cheese [Omit for V recipe.]

Preheat oven to 350°. Add a bit of extra virgin olive oil to a large frying pan and sauté the onions until translucent. Add the tomatoes and salsa and bring to a boil over medium heat. Reduce heat to low and continue to cook until mixture begins to thicken. Add beans and heat through.

Spread ⅓ of mixture into bottom of a 9"x13" baking dish. Cover with a layer of tortillas (cut into strips to cover space; does not need to be perfect). Cover with another ⅓ of bean mixture, carefully spreading to the edge of the tortillas. Sprinkle with a layer of cheese and then repeat the pattern (tortillas, bean mixture, cheese) one more time.

Bake 20-25 min. or until well heated. Top with lettuce, fresh tomatoes, avocado, olives, salsa, sour cream, etc.

> *Tip:* NOTE: You can also divide this recipe into two 8"x8" pans. This dish is also easily frozen for later use.

Chili Millet (Corn) Bread Pie (V,GF)

Thanks for the recipe, Laura!

(Recipe was adapted by Robyn.)

Preheat oven to 375°. Combine in an 9"x13" baking dish:

> 2 (15 oz.) cans chili beans (I use a red and a kidney; sometimes I do red and black)
>
> 1 C organic corn (frozen or fresh)
>
> ½ tsp. chili powder (more, if you like it hotter)
>
> ½ tsp. cayenne (more, if you like it hotter)
>
> 1 (15 oz.) can diced tomatoes with chilies (or use fresh tomatoes chopped and ½ jalapeño diced)
>
> *optional*: ½ medium onion, chopped
>
> *optional*: ¼ C cilantro, chopped

Combine in a medium bowl using a fork to be sure baking powder is evenly distributed:

> ½ tsp. sea salt
>
> 1 C millet flour (I just grind it fresh in my blender)
>
> 1 C whole-wheat flour (for gluten-free: ½ C sorghum, ½ C brown rice flour)
>
> 1 Tbsp. aluminum-free baking powder

Add to dry mixture and stir just until blended:

> 1 Tbsp. raw agave or raw honey
>
> ½ tsp. sea salt
>
> 1 C almond or rice milk
>
> 2 Tbsp. extra virgin olive oil

Spoon nine equal spoonfuls of the batter in a 3x3 pattern onto the bean mixture. Bake for 30 min. We love to serve this with lots of raw veggies, especially carrots, broccoli, and celery.

Snobby Joes (Lentils) (V)

Thanks for the recipe, Laura (adapted from happyfoody.com/2009/01/17/snobby-joes/)!

(Recipe was further adapted by Robyn.)

> 1 C uncooked lentils
> 4 C water
> 1 Tbsp. extra virgin olive oil
> 1 medium yellow onion, diced small
> 2 garlic cloves, minced
> ½ -1 Tbsp. chili powder
> 1½ tsp. dried oregano
> 1 tsp. sea salt
> 1 (8 oz.) can tomato sauce
> ¼ C tomato paste
> 3 Tbsp. real maple syrup
> 1-2 Tbsp. brown mustard
> 4-6 whole-grain rolls
> *optional*: 1 green pepper, diced small

Put the lentils in a small sauce pot and add water. Cover and bring to a boil, then reduce heat and simmer 30 min. Drain and set aside.

About 10 min. before lentils are done, sauté the onion and optional pepper in oil for 7 min. in a medium saucepan, until softened. Add the garlic and sauté a minute more.

Add the cooked lentils, the chili powder, oregano. and salt to the onion/garlic and mix. Add the tomato sauce and tomato paste. Cook about 10 min. Add the maple syrup and mustard and heat through.

Turn the heat off and let sit for about 10 min. Serve open faced, with a scoop of Snobby Joes on each half a bun.

Can also be served cold or warm in romaine lettuce leaves.

Sprouted Bean Burgers (V,GF)

Thanks for the recipe, Laura (adapted from www.sproutpeople.com/cookery/sprouted_bean_burgers.html)!

(Recipe was further adapted by Robyn.)

>   1 C adzuki sprouts
>   2 C lentil sprouts
>   1 tsp. sea salt and black pepper
>   2 Tbsp. coconut oil
>   ½ C whole-wheat flour (for gluten free: ¼ C sorghum & ¼ c garbanzo bean flour)
>   ¼ C rice milk
>   2 egg (organic, free range), slightly beaten *OR* 2 Tbsp. ground flax seeds + 6 Tbsp. water)
>   2-3 green onions, finely chopped
>   2 garlic cloves, minced
>   1 Tbsp. fresh thyme *OR* 1 tsp. dried thyme

Chop the sprouts finely or grind them in a food processor. Mix all the ingredients together and shape into thin (¼" thick) patties. Heat pan (cast iron works very well) over medium-high heat for a minute. Add oil and heat for another minute or so. Place patties in pan and brown lightly on each side. Serve on bread or bun, or in romaine or butter lettuce, garnishing to your liking. You can also freeze patties between wax paper in Ziploc bag for later use.

Zucchini Noodles, Veggies & Spicy Almond Butter Sauce (V,GF)

Thanks for the recipe, Linda (www.greenspiritliving.com)!

Noodles:

> 4 medium zucchini, peeled and cut in half

Veggies:

> 1 C bean sprouts
> 1 red bell pepper, julienned
> 1 C snow peas, halved lengthwise

Almond Butter Sauce:

> 1 C almond butter
> ½ C water
> ¼ C rice wine vinegar or coconut vinegar
> ¼ C tamari
> 3 Tbsp. fresh lime juice
> 2 Tbsp. extra virgin olive oil
> 2 tsp. crushed red pepper flakes
> 2 garlic cloves, crushed
> 2 tsp. grated fresh ginger

Garnish:

> 2 Tbsp. cilantro, minced

Transform the zucchini into noodles using a vegetable peeler or spiral slicer.

Place all the ingredients for the Almond Butter Sauce in a high-powered blender and blend until smooth. Toss the zucchini noodles and veggies with enough Almond Butter Sauce to coat well. Garnish with minced cilantro and serve immediately. *Makes 4 servings.* [See Photos section.]

> **Note:** Stored in a sealed container in the refrigerator, Almond Butter Sauce will keep for 5 days.

Raw Chalupas (R,V,GF)

Thanks for the recipe, Linda (www.rawrecipebox.blogspot.com)!

Fresh corn tortillas:

>   4 C fresh corn cut from cob
>   ½ C ground flax seeds
>   ½ C extra virgin olive oil
>   jalapeños or red peppers, to taste
>   1 tsp. sea salt

Mix all ingredients in high-powered blender. Add a little water if necessary to create a thin batter consistency (kind of like pancakes).

Spread batter on dehydrator sheets in a large circle about ¼" thick. Put in dehydrator for about 10 hrs. on 110°. Check occasionally and flip over when they are strong enough to do so. Don't let them get too crisp or you won't be able to fold them. (However, if they are crisp, they will make great tortilla chips!)

Filling:

>   1½ C raw almonds, soaked overnight and rinsed
>   ¼ C fresh lemon juice
>   2 garlic cloves
>   ½ C diced red peppers
>   ½ C diced celery
>   1 tsp. sea salt
>   ¼ C diced onion
>   2 Tbsp. water
>   2 Tbsp. cumin

Grind almonds in food processor, then add remaining ingredients and continue to process until a thick paté forms.

Assembling chalupas:

Lay corn tortilla flat and spread a thin layer of the filling on top. Add shredded romaine lettuce, chopped tomatoes, guacamole, or avocado slices, as desired. Fold tortillas in thirds and cut down the middle.

Sweet Potato Bean Burritos (V)

Thanks for the recipe, Lori!

> 1 Tbsp. extra virgin olive oil
>
> 1 onion, chopped
>
> 4 garlic cloves, minced
>
> 6 C kidney beans or your favorite beans (rinse thoroughly if canned beans are used)
>
> 2 C water
>
> 3 Tbsp. chili powder
>
> 2 tsp. ground cumin
>
> 4 tsp. prepared mustard
>
> pinch cayenne pepper, or to taste
>
> 3 Tbsp. Bragg Liquid Aminos
>
> 4 C cooked and mashed sweet potatoes
>
> 12 (10") whole-wheat flax tortillas (see *12 Steps to Whole Foods* recipe, ch. 6)
>
> 8 oz. shredded cheddar or soy/rice cheese substitute [Use soy/rice cheese for V recipe.]

Preheat oven to 350°. Heat oil in a medium skillet and sauté onion and garlic until soft. Stir in beans and mash. Gradually stir in water and heat until warm. Remove from heat and stir in the chili powder, cumin, mustard, cayenne pepper, and Bragg Liquid Aminos.

Divide bean mixture and mashed sweet potatoes evenly among the warm tortillas. Top with cheese, fold up burrito style, and place on a baking sheet. Bake for 12 min. and then serve. *Makes 12 burritos.*

Tip: Extras can be frozen for later use.

Tahini Genie Noodles (V,GF)

Thanks for the recipe, Lori Littenberg!

> 1 pkg. Udon noodles [Use wheatless Udon noodles for GF recipe.]
> 2 C assorted chopped vegetables (carrots, snap peas, leafy greens, etc.)
> sesame oil (enough to sauté veggies)
> 3 Tbsp. tahini (for a creamier sauce, add more tahini)
> ¾ C fresh apple juice (at least unsweetened, if not fresh)
> ½ tsp. umeboshi plum vinegar
> 1 tsp. Nama Shoyu

Precook noodles separately.

Sauté vegetables in a bit little sesame oil. Don't overcook—they should be crispy. (The more colorful the vegetable choices, the more appetizing the dish looks.) Add vegetables to noodles. Whisk together remaining ingredients to make the sauce. Pour sauce over the pasta and cook for three minutes. The heat will make the sauce thicken. (You can add cooked Seitan or Tofu to the dish as well, for a meat substitute.)

Black Beans & Rice (V,GF)

Thanks for the recipe, Margaret!

> 2 C cooked black or red beans (I cook 1½ C dry beans and use the leftover broth and beans for my Black Bean Soup (V,GF) on page 67)
> 3 C cooked brown basmati rice
> 2 large fresh tomatoes, diced (~ 2 C)
> ½ bunch fresh cilantro, chopped
> ½ bulb fresh garlic, chopped
> sea salt, to taste
> ½ C extra virgin olive oil, or to taste

Mix all ingredients together. Serve at room temperature and with a big green salad. Yum!

Warm Greek "Pasta" (R,V,GF)

Thanks for the recipe, Mary Gardner (of Paradise Meadows Produce) & Tom Arms

> 3 small-medium zucchinis, peeled*
> 1 garlic clove, pressed
> 2 large handfuls spinach leaves, chopped coarsely
> 2-3 Tbsp. extra virgin olive oil (or to taste)
> 4-6 basil leaves, chopped (or to taste)
> several thin slices your favorite onion
> ½ C raw kalamata olives, pitted and whole or halved (or to taste)
> 1-2 C chopped tomatoes or cherry tomatoes, halved
> sea salt and pepper, to taste
> 1 lemon, quartered
> "Rawmesan cheese"

Works best with fewer seeds, that's why we're using young zucchini. If you are using older ones, just remove the spiralized seedy part, retaining the outer "pasta" which has spiralized.

Spiralize zucchini to the width of angel hair pasta with your spiralizer (or other kitchen utensil). Put in baking dish and add salt and pepper plus a little of the olive oil, then set aside.

Stir garlic and olive oil together in a medium mixing bowl. Combine spinach, onion, tomatoes, olives, and basil with oil/garlic. Gently toss this mixture with the zucchini in the baking dish. Add more olive oil, salt, and pepper to your taste.

Heat the dish gently in a warm oven, taking care not to cook or steam the dish. This is meant to be fresh and raw, so check it often. When warm, remove and serve on warmed dinner plates. Squeeze lemon juice over the dish, then sprinkle it with the "cheese."

Quinoa Power Bowl (V,GF)

Thanks for the recipe, Meagan!

    1 C quinoa

    2 C water

    2 C chopped raw spinach

    ½ C natural peanut butter (or other nut butter)

    3 Tbsp. Bragg Amino Liquid (or more, to taste)

    2 C cooked black beans

    2 scallions, finely chopped

Cook the quinoa in the water for 8 min., then add spinach. When the water is absorbed, add the rest of the ingredients and mix until incorporated. Stir and enjoy!

Red, White, & Green Pasta (V,GF)

Thanks for the recipe, Melissa!

    ½ lb. whole-grain pasta [Use gluten-free pasta for GF recipe.]

    2 fresh tomatoes, chopped

    1 C fresh green beans

    1 Tbsp. fresh basil *OR* ½ tsp. dried basil

    ¼ C extra virgin olive oil

    1 Tbsp. balsamic vinegar

    optional: ½ C grated fresh mozzarella [Omit for V recipe.]

Blanch the green beans in boiling water for 2 min. and sift out, leaving water on the heat. Pour pasta into boiling water, cook as directed on package, then drain. In a bowl, toss the pasta with the green beans, tomatoes, mozzarella. and basil. Dress it with the olive oil and vinegar. [See Photos section.]

Three-Color Quinoa (V,GF)

Thanks for the recipe, Melissa Rubin!

> 1 C dry quinoa (⅓ C each white, red, and black)
>
> 2 C water or vegetable broth (or mixture)
>
> 2-3 leaves of 2-3 types of greens (kale, collards, chard, bok choy, mustard greens, etc.), chopped
>
> 1 butternut squash
>
> 1 Tbsp. sesame seeds
>
> fresh herbs (basil, mint, tarragon, parsley), to taste
>
> fresh garlic, minced *OR* Majestic Garlic raw vegan spread, to taste
>
> extra virgin olive oil (enough to sauté the greens)
>
> *optional*: hemp nuts or pine nuts
>
> *optional*: Maine Coast Triple Blend Flakes
>
> *optional*: nutritional yeast

Preheat oven to 375°. Put squash in the oven. (You can poke a few holes in the side facing up.) Bake for 30-50 mins.

While squash is baking, put quinoa in strainer and rinse. Add to water/broth in a sauce pan and bring to a full boil. Reduce heat, simmer for 10 mins., then remove from heat.

In a sauté pan, add garlic, basil, parsley, thyme, and olive oil (or any other spices or oil you like for flavor) and heat on medium. Add chopped greens to pan and sauté to desired texture. Take off heat, sprinkle with sesame seeds, and set aside.

When squash is done, let cool and then peel. Cut into cubes or bite-sized pieces. Put on top of greens mixture, than add quinoa and mix all together. Top with optional nuts and sprinkle with optional flakes and/or yeast.

Baked Curried Lentils (V,GF)

Thanks for the recipe, Nancy!

1 Tbsp. extra virgin olive oil

2 large (~ 1 lb.) sweet onions, chopped

2 cloves garlic, minced

1 Tbsp. curry powder (or more, to taste)

5 C vegetable broth

1 lb. (2½ C) lentils

optional: 1 C shredded white cheddar cheese (or any cheese you like) [Omit for V recipe.]

In 5-6 qt. sauce pan, sauté garlic and onions in oil. Stir over high heat until onions are tinged with brown, about 8 min. Stir in curry and broth. Sort and discard debris from lentils. Rinse lentils, drain, and put in rice cooker. Add broth mixture to lentils and cook until done. If making ahead, cool, cover, and chill up to 1 day.

Preheat oven to 350°. Pour lentils into shallow 2½ - 3 qt. greased casserole dish. Bake covered until most of liquid is absorbed, about 30 min. (if it was chilled, bake 1-1¼ hr.). Uncover, sprinkle with cheese, then bake until cheese melts. [See Photos section.]

Zucchini Cakes

Thanks for the recipe, Paula!

3 C coarsely grated zucchini

½ tsp. sea salt

1 C fresh whole-grain bread crumbs (from a baguette)

1 egg (organic and free range)

2 green onions, thinly sliced

¼ C diced bell pepper (any color)

1 Tbsp. plain yogurt

⅛ tsp. red pepper flakes

2 Tbsp. coconut oil for frying

optional: your choice of seasonings

Place zucchini in a colander, sprinkle lightly with salt and let stand 30 min. Press with paper towel to remove as much moisture as you can. It should be fairly dry, and you should have about 2 C. Place zucchini and remaining ingredients (except coconut oil) in a bowl and mix well. Form into 8 patties the size of crab cakes. Chill. Heat oil in skillet and cook patties on both sides until browned. Drain on paper towels. *Serves 4.*

Quinoa and Peas (V,GF)

Thanks for the recipe, Rae!

> 1 C quinoa
> 2 C water
> 1 pkg. loose frozen peas, defrosted
> 1 fresh lemon
> sea salt and black pepper, to taste

Rinse quinoa and cook in simmering water for 15 min., covered. Remove from stove, stir in defrosted peas, and cover. Let sit to warm the peas.

Before serving, cut lemon and squeeze over quinoa-and-pea mixture, then stir.

Add salt and pepper to taste. This is quick and easy. The lemon adds a nice tang. Other cooked or raw veggies can be substituted for or added to the peas. [See Photos section.]

Yellow Vegetable Curry (V,GF)

Thanks for the recipe, Sharon!

I know this is probably the furthest thing from an authentic curry, but I've adapted it from my favorite Thai restaurant, and I think it's pretty close. I hope you enjoy.

> 2 large carrots, cut in half and then diced
> 1 onion, diced
> 1 potato, diced
> 2 Tbsp. curry powder
> sea salt, to taste
> 1 can coconut milk
> ½ C peanut sauce (365 brand from Whole Foods)
> 1-2 Tbsp. raw agave
> 2-3 C spinach

Sauté first five ingredients in a little coconut oil until tender. You may need to add water and cover to finish the potatoes. Add the curry in at a point without water to toast it a little.

Then add next three ingredients and simmer until thickened. Remove from heat and add the spinach. Serve with your favorite grain, rice, quinoa, or couscous. [See Photos section.]

"Beefy" Portobello Veggie Pasta (V,GF)

Thanks for the recipe, Stephanie Freeman!

> 1-2 small/medium eggplants, peeled and chopped into cubes
>
> 4 large Portobello mushrooms, chopped and/or cubed
>
> 12-14 oz. cherry tomatoes
>
> 1 large white onion, chopped
>
> 3 garlic cloves, minced
>
> ¼ C pine nuts
>
> coconut oil or extra virgin olive oil
>
> sea salt
>
> black pepper
>
> 1 lb. whole-grain (wheat, quinoa, or brown rice) pasta, elbows or penne shaped
>
> *optional*: a few C spinach

Preheat oven to 350°. Place the chopped eggplant and cherry tomatoes on a nonstick baking sheet. Pour about ¼ C of the olive oil over both. Season lightly with salt and pepper and place in the oven. Roast for 20 min. or until the eggplant pieces are dark and tender and the cherry tomatoes burst.

Coat the bottom of a large sauté pan with coconut oil or olive oil. Put in the chopped onion with a little sprinkle of salt (to help release the water from the onion) and sauté. When the onions are half translucent, add the mushrooms, garlic, and optional spinach (for a green component and great taste), and continue sautéing until the onions are completely translucent. (This will flavor the mushrooms, and they will give the pasta a hearty flavor and you will never miss the beef!)

When the eggplant and tomatoes are finished roasting, add them to the sauté pan. Squish the tomatoes a bit for a more juicy sauce (if needed, add ⅓ - ½ C water from pasta or ⅓ C low-sodium veggie broth). Then add the pine nuts.

Cook the pasta, drain, and add to the sauce. Stir well to incorporated everything together, then pour into a large bowl or platter and serve! *Makes about 5-6 servings.*

Beno's Beans and Rice (V,GF)

Thanks for the recipe, Steve "Beno" Levine!

> 1 can black or red beans, rinsed and drained
> 1-1½ C shelled edamame, fresh or frozen
> 1 bunch green onions, chopped
> 1 can sliced water chestnuts, drained
> 1 C corn (fresh, frozen, or canned/rinsed)
> 2 red, yellow, or green bell peppers, seeded and chopped
> 1 habañero pepper, seeded and chopped
> 1 bunch cilantro, rinsed and chopped
> 3 C cooked brown rice
> 1 avocado, peeled and sliced (8-16 pieces)
> mango salsa, to taste

Toss first nine ingredients in a salad bowl. Serve with avocado and salsa. *Makes about 8 servings.*

Favorite Pasta (V)

Thanks for the recipe, Tara!

> 1 lb. whole-grain pasta (such as rotini or penne)
> 2 C fresh mushrooms, sliced
> ½ C raw sunflower seeds
> 2 garlic cloves, minced
> whole-wheat flour
> 2 C finely chopped broccoli
> 1 (28 oz.) can tomato chunks
> 1-2 Tbsp extra virgin olive oil (for sautéing)
> sea salt, to taste
> black pepper, to taste
> *optional*: ¼ C shredded Parmesan cheese

Cook pasta. While pasta is cooking, sauté mushrooms, sunflower seeds, and garlic in oil. Add a little flour to thicken. Add broccoli and tomatoes., then season with salt and pepper. Drain pasta, toss into sauté pan, and mix all together well. Optionally serve with a sprinkling of Parmesan cheese.

Sesame Noodles (V,GF)

Thanks for the recipe, Tara!

> 1 lb. whole-grain noodles, cooked [Use gluten-free noodles for GF recipe.]
> ⅓ C tahini
> 2 Tbsp. almond or peanut butter
> 1 tsp. raw agave or real maple syrup
> 2 tsp. brown-rice vinegar
> 2 tsp. tamari or Nama Shoyu
> 1 tsp. toasted sesame oil
> 1½ tsp. coriander
> 1 Tbsp. water, or to desired consistency

Blend sauce ingredients together in blender until creamy. Pour over noodles and toss gently. Leftover sauce freezes well.

Variation: Omit water, half the amount of tamari, and double the amount of nut butter. Serve as a dip or spread for vegetables or crackers.

Southern Red Beans and Rice (V,GF)

Thanks for the recipe, Tara!

> 4 C cooked red beans
> 1 C reserved cooking liquid from beans
> 1 onion, chopped
> 2-3 celery ribs, chopped
> 1 green pepper, chopped
> 2 garlic cloves, crushed
> 1½ tsp. thyme
> 1-2 bay leaves
> dash cayenne pepper, to taste
> salt and pepper, to taste
> sliced avocado, for garnish
> *optional*: arrow root powder

Sauté vegetables in a little oil, beginning with onion. Add a bit of water to pan to prevent garlic from burning. When vegetables are soft, add seasonings, red beans, and enough cooking liquid to moisten. Thicken with a bit of arrowroot powder, if desired. Simmer for 15 min. to allow flavors to blend. *Remove bay leaf!* Serve over brown rice, with sliced avocado on top. [See Photos section.]

Cado Fajitas (V,GF)

Thanks for the recipe, Tiffany!

Note: This recipe is gluten free only if you use corn tortillas.

1 Tbsp. extra virgin olive oil
8-10 sliced mushrooms
¾ C lightly chopped cilantro
½ red bell pepper, sliced
½ green bell pepper, sliced
½ yellow bell pepper, sliced
½ C chopped Roma tomato
¼ C chopped yellow onion
sea salt, to taste
Tabasco, to taste

Combine all ingredients in a medium-sized skillet. Slice up some ripe organic avocado and layer on an organic whole-wheat tortillas. Then top with fajita mixture and enjoy. No meat, cheese, or sour cream is necessary, trust me! [See Photos section.]

Side Dishes

Side Dishes

Anna's Sweet Hash "Partatoes" (V,GF)

Thanks for the recipe, Anna!

> parsnips (desired amount)
> sweet potatoes (desired amount)
> raw ginger, finely grated (to taste)
> coconut oil *OR* coconut butter (for sautéing)
> sea salt, to taste

Grate the parsnips and potatoes as you would for hash browns. Sauté in coconut oil/butter with sea salt. Enjoy! [See Photos section.]

Collard Green Rolls with Peanut Sauce (V,GF)

Thanks for the recipe, Anonymous!

½ C cilantro, loosely packed and roughly chopped

½ C fresh fennel, finely chopped

1 handful fresh basil, chopped

1 handful fresh mint, chopped

½ C grated carrot

½ C thinly sliced cucumber sticks, about 2" long

½ C thinly sliced red bell pepper sticks, 2" long

1 package tempeh, cut into 2" strips

tamari, to taste

1½ tsp. extra virgin coconut oil

1 bunch collard greens

Fill a sauté pan with ½" water and place a steamer basket in the pan. Place 1 collard leaf at a time into the steaming saute pan for 4-5 min. with a lid over the pan. You want the leaves to be supple enough to roll—the thick vein in the middle needs to be bendable without breaking. Once you have them all steamed, place them to the side to cool.

Place coconut oil in a sauté pan (same one is OK). Once the oil melts, put in the tempeh, sprinkle with tamari, and cook the tempeh until crunchy. Once crunchy and brown, put it to the side to cool.

Chop remaining veggies and herbs.

Place one cooled collard leaf onto a cutting board and prepare your roll with all ingredients. Layer ingredients onto the collard leaf, off center and closest to you, creating a smile-like shape on the leaf. Pull the end of the leaf over the filling, then fold both sides over toward the center, like a burrito. While gently pulling it toward you, roll the collard leaf away from you. Repeat for other rolls. Cut rolls in half and drizzle peanut sauce over the top to serve.

Carol's Kale (V,GF)

Thanks for the recipe, Carol Pacheco!

>3 C finely chopped kale
>
>½ C extra virgin olive oil
>
>½ tsp. sea salt (or more, to taste)
>
>1½ C raisins
>
>1½ C soaked/sprouted sunflower seeds or chopped soaked almonds (sprouted for 1 day)

Put kale in the S blade food processor and finely chop. Mix all together and refrigerate. This also tastes great with Trader Joe's Goddess dressing.

Tabouli (R,V,GF)

Thanks for the recipe, Elizabeth!

>1 bunch parsley
>
>1 bunch cilantro
>
>1 handful chopped herbs (I use basil almost exclusively in this)
>
>2 scallions
>
>2 handfuls grape tomatoes
>
>¼ - ⅓ C hemp seeds
>
>2 Tbsp. extra virgin olive oil *OR* 1 Tbsp. flaxseed oil
>
>1 Tbsp. fresh lemon or lime juice
>
>sea salt, to taste
>
>sprinkle cayenne pepper

Chop parsley and cilantro (save stems for juice or smoothies). Add to a bowl with chopped herbs. Slice scallions (use a bit of the green part too) and add to greens in bowl. Slice grape tomatoes in half and add. Add hemp seeds, oil, citrus juice, salt, and cayenne, and then toss. Taste and adjust seasonings if needed.

>**Note:** The hemp seeds stand in for cracked wheat and give the salad a boost of protein. I like to have this with homemade hummus and, for those who eat dairy, tzitziki made with goat's milk yogurt, chopped or grated cucumber, garlic, chopped mint, sea salt, and pepper.

Broccoli Tabouli (R,V,GF)

Thanks for the recipe, Emily!

Veggies:

> 1 C broccoli, cut into small pieces
>
> 3 green onions, thinly sliced
>
> ½ C fresh cilantro, finely minced
>
> 1 cucumber, small diced
>
> 1 C fresh parsley, finely minced
>
> 1 celery stalk, finely diced
>
> ½ red pepper, finely diced

Dressing:

> juice of 2 lemons
>
> ½ C extra virgin olive oil
>
> ½ tsp. sea salt
>
> ½ tsp. curry
>
> ½ tsp. cumin
>
> 1 jalapeño pepper, seeded and finely diced
>
> 1 garlic clove, pressed

Mix dressing ingredients together, pour over veggies, and toss well. Allow to marinate for 30 min. to combine flavors.

Tangy Steamed Kale (V,GF)

Thanks for the recipe, Jamie!

> 2 C kale
> 2 Tbsp. tahini
> 5 tsp. fresh lemon juice
> 2 tsp. Bragg Liquid Aminos [Use tamari for GF recipe.]
> 1 tsp. apple cider vinegar
> 1 garlic clove, crushed in press
> 1 tsp. nutritional yeast
> water (to thin if desired)

Wash and then blot, shake, or spin dry the kale. Tear it into smallish pieces and lightly steam so it is still a nice, bright green.

Whisk all other ingredients together to make the dressing. Brown rice to serve kale over, if desired. *Makes 1 serving.* [See Photos section.]

> *Tip:* When my husband and I make a full meal out of this, I cook up about 1-1½ C of brown rice, an 8 qt. pot full of kale, and 3-4 times the dressing. The kale does shrink a lot when steamed, so be prepared for a great reduction in size.

Muesli (V,GF)

Thanks for the recipe, Jenna Strawn!

12 oz. apple juice concentrate, thawed

48 oz. water

1 C raw sliced almonds

½ C raw sunflower seeds

½ C raw chopped pecans

½ C raw sesame seeds

1 C raisins

1 C coconut flakes, natural

1 lb. berries, peaches, apples, apricots, etc. (fresh or frozen)

1 Tbsp. cinnamon or coriander

6 C uncooked regular oats [Use gluten-free oats for GF recipe.]

2 C rolled uncooked multi-grain blend

1 C flax seed meal, freshly ground

1 C raw wheat germ

Mix all together in a large bowl that has a lid. Keep covered in the refrigerator.

> **Note:** We really like this. Doesn't need sweetener. Can substitute cranberries for raisins, or use a combination. I usually use apples for the fruit. If you don't have multi-grain blend, just use 8 C oats instead of 6 C. You could substitute other frozen juices if desired. We tried adding 1 can crushed pineapple with juice, but it didn't make much difference in the flavor—not enough return for the cost of the fruit. Lasts up to a week, but is at its peak for the first 3-4 days. After it starts getting too mushy, scoop it out onto dehydrator sheets and let it dry into "cookies." Yum, yum!

Roasted Broccoli (V,GF)

Thanks for the recipe, Jessica!

1 lb. broccoli florets, separated

1" piece fresh ginger root, peeled and finely grated (I use a microplane)

1 garlic clove, minced

½ tsp. sea salt

pinch cayenne

1-2 Tbsp. extra virgin olive oil

black pepper, to taste

Preheat oven to 400°. Place all ingredients except broccoli in a mixing bowl and stir with a fork. Add broccoli and combine until broccoli is well coated. Place broccoli on a baking sheet and roast until tender, about 12 min. (test with a fork). Serve warm or at room temperature.

Stuffed Avocados from the Ozarks (R,V,GF)

Thanks for the recipe, Judith!

> 6 avocados
>
> 1 qt. alfalfa sprouts
>
> ¼ - 1¼ C cucumber juice
>
> 1-5 garlic cloves
>
> ¼ - ¼ C green onions, chopped
>
> ¼ - 2 C cashew seed yogurt or presoaked (and drained) sesame seeds
>
> 1 Tbsp. + ½ tsp. brown miso
>
> ¼ - 1 Tbsp. fresh lemon juice
>
> ⅛ tsp. cayenne (or less, if you like less heat)

Blend all but the avocados and sprouts together until smooth. Generously toss sprouts and blended sauce together to create the filling (reserve some sauce and sprouts separately, as topping).

Cut avocados in half. Remove pits and scoop each avocado half out from its "shell" in one piece. Stuff the avocado halves with filling. Place stuffed avocados on romaine lettuce and top with leftover reserved sauce and sprouts.

Avocado Quinoa Bowl (V,GF)

Thanks for the recipe, Kandace!

1 jalapeño pepper, diced
1 onion, diced
5 cloves garlic, finely diced or crushed
2 Tbsp red wine vinegar
2½ C cooked black beans
¼ C extra virgin olive oil
sea salt, to taste
black pepper, to taste
4 C cooked quinoa
2 avocados, diced
2-4 tomatoes, diced
cilantro, to taste
1 can olives, sliced

Prepare quinoa as usual until soft and fluffy. Meanwhile, sauté jalapeño, onion, and garlic in the red wine vinegar. Add black beans. Remove from heat. Add olive oil to the cooked quinoa and salt and pepper to taste. Combine quinoa and bean mixture in serving bowls. Top with avocados, tomatoes, olives, and cilantro.

Green Fajita Rice (V,GF)

Thanks for the recipe, Kandace!

½ C vegetable broth
1 C spinach leaves
½ C cilantro
4 green onions
cooked brown rice

Blend first four ingredients in a high-powered blender. Pour over the top of cooked brown rice and serve alone or with Fajitas.

Curried Couscous (V)

Thanks for the recipe, Lori!

> 1-2 tsp. extra virgin olive oil
> 1 large onion, chopped
> 1 C sliced carrots
> 2 garlic cloves, pressed or very finely chopped
> 1-2 tsp. curry powder
> 1 C broth
> 1 C whole-wheat couscous
> *optional*: ½ tsp. sea salt
> *optional*: craisins or other dried fruit
> *optional*: yogurt [Omit for V recipe.]
> *optional*: chutney

Sauté onion, carrots, and garlic in olive oil for 5 min. Stir in curry and optional salt. Add broth and bring to boil, then cover and simmer for 5-7 min. or until carrots are tender. Stir in couscous and optional dried fruit, cover, and remove from heat. Let stand 5 min., then fluff with a fork. Optionally serve with yogurt and/or chutney.

Roasted Root Vegetable Mash (V,GF)

Thanks for the recipe, Mallory!

1 parsnip

1 rutabaga

1 turnip

1 sweet potato

1 small (or ½ larger) sweet onion

1 head garlic

1 large carrot

2 Tbsp. extra virgin olive oil

⅓ C vegetable broth

⅓ C coconut milk (or other such as almond or rice)

2 Tbsp. Vegan Butter (I use Earth Balance) or Vegan Mayo (they both work great)

sea salt

black pepper

Preheat oven to 350°. Cut all the veggies up into similar-sized cubes. Keep in mind that the smaller you cut them, the faster they will cook.

Peel the garlic and put everything into the roasting pan and toss in olive oil. Roast in the oven until the vegetables start to caramelize and get much darker (if you see some black crispy spots, it's perfect).

It usually takes about 45 min., but cooking time will depend on the size you cut your veggies. When your veggies are almost done, put the remaining ingredients into a sauce pan and slightly heat. Then put all your roasted veggies into your high-powered blender and add some of the liquid and blend. Add more liquid until you reach the consistency you like. You can also mash by hand, if you prefer the rustic look. *Makes about 4 servings.*

Sweet Potato Fries (GF)

Thanks for the recipe, Mary!

> 1 sweet potato
> 1 Tbsp. butter
> 1 Tbsp. coconut oil

Slice sweet potato into ¼" slices. Pan fry the sweet potato slices over medium heat in butter and oil. Once slightly brown, turn down the heat and cover, cooking until tender. *Makes 1 serving.*

Middle Eastern Fried Farina (V)

Thanks for the recipe, Richard Taormino's Grandmother!

> 7-7½ C water (exact measurements are critical)
> ½ C raw coconut sugar
> 1 stick butter *OR* ½ C extra virgin olive oil
> 1 C faina
> ground cinnamon (for garnish)

In a 3 qt. or larger pot that has a tight-fitting lid, add coconut sugar to water and bring water to rapid rolling boil.

In a large non-stick fry pan, melt the butter/oil until sizzling, then add farina and keep pan relatively hot to insure high-temperature requirement. Toast the farina stirring constantly; try to have farina and water at high temps, but careful not to burn farina!

Now combine contents of fry pan into pot with rapid boiling water, stir well, shut off the heat, and cover tightly. Keep covered for approximately 10 to 12 min. Then remove lid and stir well.

Put farina mixture into individual bowls and garnish with cinnamon. For extra zing, melt string cheese in the bowls you put farina in. *Makes 4 servings.*

> *Tip:* To use as a light main dish, serve with pita bread and cantaloupe on the side.

Broccoli and Peas (R,GF)

Thanks for the recipe, Sherry!

    1 C peas (fresh or frozen/thawed)

    1 C broccoli, cut to the size of the peas

    8 grape tomatoes

    ¼ C honey mustard dressing (equal parts honey, grainy mustard, water, and extra virgin olive oil)

    seasonings, to taste (I use kelp and dulse flakes, cayenne, and garlic)

    1 Tbsp. pine nuts (for garnish)

Mix all main ingredients thoroughly and garnish with pine nuts.

Mary's "Rice Pilaf" (R,V,GF)

Thanks for the recipe, Mary Gardner (of Paradise Meadows Produce) and Tom Arms!

Love savory rice pilaf? This is a raw version that uses colorful and sweet garnet yams in place of the cooked rice. You can adjust the size of the yams and the spices to your taste.

> 2 smallish-medium garnet yams
> 1-2 Tbsp. coarsely chopped fresh onion
> ½ C water
> ½ C raisins
> ⅓ - ½ C kalamata olives, pitted and chopped
> 2-3 Tbsp. avocado oil
> 1 to 2 Tbsp. mustard seed (whole)
> 1 tsp. ground cinnamon
> 1 tsp. ground coriander
> ¼ tsp. ground cloves or 4+ whole cloves
> sea salt, to taste
> black pepper, to taste
> *optional*: 1-2 Tbsp. nutritional yeast powder or flakes (per serving)

Preheat oven to 250°. Peel the yams and cut into pieces that your food processor can handle. Put the onion with the yam pieces into your food processor fitted with the S blade. Process until the yams turn into a rice-like consistency. (You may have to process in several batches, depending on your processor size.)

Put processed yam/onion mixture into a large, flat baking dish. Add water, raisins, and olives and mix into pilaf. Add oil and spices and stir well so all is mixed into the pilaf.

Place uncovered baking dish into oven. Pilaf should be gently warmed in about ½ hour. However, test it at 10 and 20 min. to avoid cooking or steaming. You should be able to stick your finger into the pilaf without getting burned.

Sprinkle with salt and pepper and optional nutritional yeast, and enjoy! *Makes 4-5 1-cup servings.*

Tip: Keeps up to 1 week in a glass container in refrigerator. May also be served cold.

Baked Rice and Veggies (V,GF)

Thanks for the recipe, Tina!

1 can coconut milk
1 can water + 1 tsp. veg. broth powder
⅓ C yogurt or kefir
1 bag frozen mixed vegetables
1½ C instant whole-grain brown rice
1 onion, chopped *OR* 1 tsp. onion powder
black pepper, to taste
sea salt, to taste
paprika, to taste

Preheat oven to 375°. Stir all together in a 9"x13" dish. Cover and bake for 45 min. Then take cover off and bake for another 10 min.

Chili, Soups, Stews, & Sandwiches

Chili

Vegetarian Chili (Chili Sin Carne) (V,GF)

Thanks for the recipe, Garon!

(Recipe was adapted by Robyn.)

½ -1 large onion, diced

3-4 small zucchini, diced

2 banana peppers, seeded and chopped *OR* 5-6 sweet peppers, chopped

1 large green pepper, seeded and chopped

3-4 celery stalks, chopped

1 Tbsp. minced garlic *OR* 2 garlic cloves, pressed

1 tsp. cumin

1 tsp. oregano

2 cans stewed tomatoes (Italian)

1 can black beans

1 can white beans

1 can kidney beans

2 C frozen corn

¼ C raw agave, coconut palm sugar, or Sucanat

1 Tbsp. vegetarian chili seasoning

sea salt and black pepper, to taste

Sauté onion, peppers, and celery in large sauce pan with a little coconut oil. Add tomatoes (if they are whole, I like to blend some for just a few seconds), beans, and seasoning. Simmer for 30 min. Taste and adjust seasoning as desired. Then add zucchini and cook 20-30 min. You may need to add extra water, depending on desired consistency.

I also like to buy dry mixed beans (Costco, Good Earth, Sunflower Market), soak them overnight, cook them, and then use for the chili. Makes it taste better and is better for you, but definitely takes more planning ahead and prep time.

Vegetarian Chili with Cashews and Kale (V,GF)

Thanks for the recipe, Jill!

(Recipe was adapted by Robyn.)

Prep time: 15-32 min. Cook time: 30-40 min.

1 Tbsp. extra virgin olive oil

1 yellow onion, finely diced

2-3 garlic cloves, minced

1 pkg. tempeh, seitan, or tofu, chopped [Use tofu or gluten-free tempeh for GF recipe.]

1 tsp. dried oregano

2 Tbsp. chili powder

1 tsp. ground cumin

¼ tsp. ground cinnamon

½ tsp. cayenne pepper

1 tsp. sea salt

3½ C vegetable broth

2 Tbsp. tomato paste

1 can (15.8 oz.) kidney beans, drained

1 can (15.8 oz.) black beans, drained

1 can (16 oz.) diced tomatoes with mild green chilies

1 C colored bell pepper, seeded and diced

1 C small zucchini or yellow summer squash, sliced into half rounds

1 C kale, stemmed and chopped or torn into bite-sized pieces

1 carrot, grated

¼ C raw cashews, chopped

½ C chopped fresh cilantro

optional: 1-2 Tbsp. fresh lime juice (optional, but delicious)

In a large frying pan, heat the oil over medium heat. Add onion and garlic and sauté until translucent, about 5 min. Add seitan, tofu, or tempeh and cook until browned, about 3 min. Add oregano, chili powder, cumin, cinnamon, cayenne pepper, and salt and sauté for 2 min.

Stir in broth and tomato paste, then add kidney beans, black beans, tomatoes, bell pepper, zucchini or squash, kale, and carrot. Bring to a simmer, reduce the heat to low, cover, and cook for about 20 min., stirring occasionally. Add the cashews and cook for 5-7 min. Sprinkle with cilantro and optional lime juice just before serving. Makes 8 servings.

Veggie Chili (V,GF)

Thanks for the recipe, Pam!

The great part of this recipe is that this is a basic ingredient list and you can easily add or subtract any ingredients according to your taste.

1 onion, chopped
2-3 garlic cloves, minced
1 pepper, chopped
1 zucchini, chopped
1 large carrot, sliced
1 small package mushrooms
1 small package grape tomatoes
1 can or equivalent cannellini beans
1 can kidney beans
1 can lima beans
1 can tomato paste or purée
chili powder, to taste
sea salt and black pepper, to taste
optional: red pepper flakes or chili seasoning

Sauté the first seven ingredients until onions are clear, then simmer until veggies are crisp-tender. Then add beans and heat through. You can add more tomato purée if desired. Enjoy!!

Soups

Minestrone Soup (V,GF)

Thanks for the recipe, Alina!

(Recipe was adapted by Robyn.)

½ C dried kidney or garbanzo beans *OR* 4 C canned kidney or garbanzo beans

2 Tbsp. extra virgin olive oil

1 large onion, chopped

3 celery stalks, sliced

2 garlic cloves, finely chopped or pressed

4 C water

3-4 tsp. Better Than Bouillon

2 tsp. dried basil *OR* 2 Tbsp. chopped fresh basil leaves

1 qt. canned tomatoes, broken up

½ (6 oz.) can tomato paste

½ C whole-grain shell macaroni (uncooked)

2 medium carrots, pared and sliced

2 medium zucchini, chopped

optional: 1 C chopped spinach (fresh or frozen)

If using dried beans, cover beans with water in large saucepan, refrigerate overnight, then drain. (Or to quick-soak beans, bring to a boil in water over high heat, cook 2 min., remove from heat and let stand one hour, then drain.)

In large saucepan, heat oil over medium heat. Add onion and celery. Sauté, stirring occasionally, for 8-10 min. or until tender. Add garlic and optional spinach and sauté, stirring occasionally, for 2-3 min.

Add water, Better Than Bouillon, beans, and basil. Bring to a boil over high heat. Lower heat, cover, and simmer 1 hr. Add tomatoes, tomato paste, and dry pasta. Return to boil. (Add more water at this point if you like a more brothy soup.) Lower heat, cover, and simmer 5-7 min. or until pasta is partially cooked. Add carrots, simmer for 5 more min. Add zucchini and spinach and simmer for an additional 5 min. or until carrots and zucchini are crisp-tender; do not overcook vegetables. Serve. *Preparation time: 20 min. Cooking time: 1 hr. 20 min.* [See Photos section.]

Rainy Day Lentil Soup (V,GF)

Thanks for the recipe, Amy A.!

2 C lentils, uncooked

8 C water or vegetable stock

1 medium onion, chopped

2 small carrots, thickly sliced

1 celery rib, chopped

1 large potato, peeled and cut into large cubes

2 bay leaves

1 vegetable (no-MSG) bouillon or Better Than Bouillon (only if water is used instead of stock) [Use gluten-free bouillon or BTB for GF recipe.]

1 tsp. crushed coriander

½ tsp. cumin

freshly ground pepper, to taste

2 garlic cloves, minced

sea salt, to taste

2-4 oz. fresh spinach (chopped, if large leaves)

2 tsp. red wine vinegar

Pick over the lentils and wash/drain.

Start the water or stock heating in the pressure cooker while you chop the vegetables. Add all ingredients except the garlic, salt, spinach, and vinegar into the cooker and bring to a boil. Seal the cooker and cook at high pressure for 10 min. Remove from heat and allow to sit for 5 min. before using a quick-release method to release the pressure. (If you don't have a pressure cooker, you can simply cook this on the stove until the lentils are tender, about1 hr.)

Check to make sure the lentils and potatoes are tender; if not, cook covered but not at pressure until done, adding water if it seems too thick. Add the garlic, salt, and spinach and check the seasonings, adding more cumin and coriander as needed. Cook for just a couple of minutes to wilt the spinach. Stir in the vinegar at the end, then serve. *Makes 6 servings.*

Celeriac Soup (V,GF)

Thanks for the recipe, Beverly Graddy!

> juice of 2 lemons
> 1 fist-sized celeriac (celery root), peeled and coarsely chopped
> ¼ C shallots, coarsely chopped
> 1 tsp. sea salt
> 4 C water
> ¼ C extra virgin olive oil

Place everything except oil in a blender and process until very smooth. Strain through fine-mesh strainer or nut milk bag. Whisk in the oil slowly. Adjust seasoning to taste, adding a bit more lemon juice or salt as you like.

Bean & Barley Soup (V)

Thanks for the recipe, Christine!

(Recipe was adapted by Robyn.)

> 2 tsp. extra virgin olive oil
> 1 C chopped onion
> 1 C finely chopped carrot
> ¼ C chopped celery
> 8 C organic vegetable broth
> ¼ tsp. crushed red pepper
> 6 garlic cloves, crushed or 3 tsp. minced
> 2 4" rosemary sprigs
> 1 (19-oz.) can dark red kidney beans, rinsed and drained, divided
> 1 C fresh tomatoes chopped
> 1 C uncooked barley
> 10 C (about 10 oz.) fresh spinach leaves, torn
> ¼ tsp. freshly ground black pepper

Measure 1 C beans and mash with a fork in a small bowl. Reserve remaining whole beans. Heat oil in pan over medium heat. Add onion, carrot, and celery and cook 4 min. Add broth, red pepper, garlic, rosemary, mashed beans, whole beans, and barley. Bring to a boil, then reduce heat and simmer on medium to medium-low for 35 min. or until barley is tender. Remove rosemary sprigs. Stir in spinach, tomatoes,and black pepper and cook 5 min or until barley is tender. *Makes 8 servings.*

Wintry Coconut-Veggie Soup (V,GF)

Thanks for the recipe, Dawn the Detox Diva!

> 6 C veggie broth
> 2 large cans coconut milk
> 2 tsp. sea salt
> 1 C almond milk (unsweetened)
> 1 C cubed new potatoes (more if desired)
> 2 C chopped cabbage
> 1 C sliced carrots
> 1 large garlic clove, finely minced or pressed
> ½ C chopped onions
> ½ C chopped celery
> 6-8 C packed fresh spinach, roughly chopped
> 1 tsp. Spice Hunter Thai Seasoning mix (very important!)
> juice of 2 fresh limes

In a large soup pot add the first 7 ingredients and simmer 40 min.

In a separate pan, sauté garlic, onions, and celery. Then add spinach and briefly sauté some more.

Add the sautéed ingredients and Thai seasoning mix to the soup mixture. Squeeze fresh limes into soup (either while cooking and/or at end). Simmer for an addition 30 min. and serve.

Thai Tomato Soup (V,GF)

Thanks for the recipe, Debbie Gordon!

> 1 young coconut (use both water and meat)
> 2 C coconut water
> ½ C water
> 1 C lettuce mix
> ½ red pepper
> 2 medium tomatoes *OR* 2 small handfuls grape tomatoes
> 2 scallions
> 3 small garlic cloves
> ½ C loosely packed cilantro
> 2 Tbsp. Bragg Liquid Aminos
> 1 heaping Tbsp. raw sesame tahini
> 2 Tbsp. flaxseed oil
> tiny sprinkle cayenne pepper
> 1 Tbsp. kelp and dulse
> 1-2 avocados, peeled and pitted

Blend all ingredients in a blender. Serve over diced avocado. *Makes 4 servings.* [See Photos section.]

Clam Chowder (GF)

Thanks for the recipe, DiAnne!

> 3 (6 oz.) cans clams
> 6 C diced yellow potatoes
> 1 C diced celery
> 1 C onion diced fine
> 2 C plain almond or rice milk
> ¼ - ⅓ C raw cashews
> 1½ tsp. sea salt
> black pepper, to taste

Put vegetables in a pot, pour juice off clams onto vegetables, and finish covering with water. Boil until tender. Remove 2 C of cooked vegetables and put in high-powered blender along with milk, cashews, and salt. Blend until thick and smooth. Return to the pot with the rest of the cooked vegetables. Add the clams and black pepper; also adjust taste with more salt if needed.

Melissa's Green Soup (V,GF)

Thanks for the recipe, Dorothy!

> 3 C chicken or vegetable broth [Use gluten-free broth for GF recipe.]
> ¾ C chopped cauliflower
> ¾ C chopped broccoli
> ½ onion, chopped
> 1 tsp. chopped ginger
> 2 tsp. chopped garlic
> extra virgin olive oil (for sautéing)
> 10 button mushrooms
> 2½ C packed baby spinach

Cook first six ingredients together about 15 min. While that's cooking, sauté the mushrooms in olive oil, then add the spinach to the pan and cook down a bit. Then purée everything together in blender. Delicious and so creamy!

Thai Coconut Corn Soup (V,GF)

Thanks for the recipe, Evi from Germany!

1 Tbsp. extra virgin olive oil

3 garlic cloves, minced

4 scallions (white and green parts), thinly sliced diagonally

1 red bell pepper, cut into short, narrow strips

1 C chopped bok choy

2 (15 oz.) cans light coconut milk

2 C rice milk

1 (16 oz.) bag frozen corn

2 tsp. curry powder

1 tsp. sea salt

½ C minced fresh cilantro, for a garish

optional: ¼ tsp. Thai red curry paste (more or less, to taste), dissolved in a little water

Heat the oil in a small soup pot. Add the garlic, white parts of the scallions, and the bell pepper. Sauté over medium-low heat until softened and golden, about 2-3 min. Add the coconut milk, rice milk, corn, curry powder, green parts of the scallions, and optional curry paste. Bring to a rapid simmer and then lower the heat. Cover and simmer gently for 5 min. Season with salt and remove from the heat. Serve, passing around the cilantro for topping. *Makes 6 servings.*

Spinach Protein Soup (V,GF)

Thanks for the recipe, H. Raven Rose!

This super-quick-to-make, filling, single-serving soup is creamy and delicious, alkalizing and protein packed and, at under 200 calories, a convenient healthful food option.

16 oz. frozen spinach

1 scoop Natural SunWarrior protein powder

optional: a bit of extra virgin olive oil

optional: sea salt or other fresh or dried herbs, such as oregano, to your taste

Heat spinach. Then put it in a blender with a scoop of protein powder and any optional ingredients, then blend until smooth. Adjust seasonings, if desired, and serve up hot!

Raw Cream of Celery Soup (R,V,GF)

Thanks for the recipe, Jon!

2-3 celery stalks

1 small bunch parsley

juice of 1-2 lemons *OR* 3-4 Tbsp, raw apple cider vinegar

¼ - ½ C extra virgin olive oil

½ large avocado

8-16 oz. filtered water, at room temperature

Bragg Liquid Aminos, to taste

real maple syrup (grade B) *OR* raw honey, to taste

fresh basil, to taste (less is more)

optional: 1-2 garlic cloves

optional: ½ C (or more) sprouts

optional: ½ C raisins or goji berries

optional: very small piece serrano pepper, for a little kick (for me, ¼" - ½")

Blend all the above in high-powered blender until creamy. After blending the soup, you can optionally add diced tomatoes or sun-dried tomatoes and/or pine nuts (as a garnish to the bowls).

Leslee's Roasted Cauliflower-Vegetable-Split Pea Soup (V,GF)

Thanks for the recipe, Leslee!

Buy organic everything whenever possible!

> 2 heads cauliflower, cut in 1" florets
>
> 1 large sweet potato, cut into bite-sized pieces
>
> 3 garlic cloves, minced
>
> 1 large yellow onion, sliced in half & cut very fine
>
> 6 carrots, cut into bite-sized pieces
>
> 4 celery stalks, diced
>
> 1 head broccoli, cut into 1" florets
>
> extra virgin olive oil (enough to lightly coat all vegetables)
>
> 1½ C split peas, rinsed & soaked at least 1 hour & drained
>
> 2-3 qt. organic vegetable stock (not broth)
>
> sea salt, to taste
>
> black pepper, to taste
>
> minced fresh ginger, to taste

Preheat oven to 350°. In a large roasting pan, toss all vegetables except peas with olive oil to lightly coat all. Roast in oven for about 25-30 min. or until golden brown.

Put all roasted vegetables and the peas in a large stock pot with enough vegetable stock to cover all. Bring to a boil, then simmer for 30 min. or until cauliflower is very tender. Use a stick blender and purée all vegetables—or leave some chunks in it if you like chunky soup. If you don't have a stick blender (the fastest and easiest way to purée soups right in their pots while hot), you can purée the soup in batches in a blender when it is cooled down; then just reheat the soup. After soup is blended, add salt, pepper, and ginger to taste (I start with a 1" piece and work up from there). Enjoy!

Creamy Cauliflower Soup (V,GF)

Thanks for the recipe, Linda (lindasgoldenyears.blogspot.com)!

(Recipe was adapted by Robyn.)

> 1 head cauliflower
> 1 onion
> 1 Tbsp. sea salt
> 3-4 Tbsp. extra virgin olive oil
> 3-4 Tbsp. oat flour [Use gluten-free flour for GF recipe.]
> 2-3 C almond milk
> *optional*: cheese or cashew cream, as garnish [Omit cheese for V recipe.]

Boil the first three ingredients until soft. Drain, reserving liquid. Blend veggies together. Make a white sauce by heating the oil on medium heat, adding the flour, and stirring in the milk. Whisk until the mixture thickens; be sure it does not boil after you add the milk! Combine the blended veggies and white sauce, and there's your soup. If you need to thin it out at all, add some of the reserved vegetable liquid. Serve with or without cheese/cashew cream.

Cauliflower-Spinach Soup (V,GF)

Thanks for the recipe, Lynn!

> 3-4 garlic cloves, crushed
> 1 onion, chopped
> 3-4 celery stalks, celery
> extra virgin olive oil (just enough for sautéing)
> 1 qt. organic vegetable broth
> 1 head cauliflower, roughly chopped
> 16 oz. spinach
> 2+ C almond milk
> 1-2 tsp. sea salt
> *optional*: 3 shakes cayenne pepper

Sauté the garlic, onion, and celery in the oil. Add broth to mixture, then add cauliflower and simmer lightly for just a few minutes. Add almond milk, salt, optional pepper, and spinach, then remove from heat. Let spinach wilt (not cooking it to death). When spinach has wilted, purée in your blender in three separate batches.

Can top with chopped onions & tomatoes or hemp seeds. I recently topped with chopped Teriyaki Almonds (in chapter 7 of *12 Steps to Whole Foods*). Was wonderful! Makes a nice baked potato topping and goes nicely with a veggie wrap.

Black Bean Soup (V,GF)

Thanks for the recipe, Margaret!

> 2-2½ C cooked black beans (including broth created by cooking them)
> 1 C vegetable broth (or more for a more "brothy" soup)
> 1 medium yellow onion, chopped
> ½ bunch fresh cilantro
> 6 garlic cloves, cut into halves
> 1 can organic diced tomatoes (the fire-roasted tomatoes are extra special)
> 2 tsp. cumin
> 1 Tbsp. chili powder
> 1 Tbsp. oregano
> sea salt, to taste

Combine all ingredients and simmer until onions are soft or for about 20 min. Serve with organic corn chips or rice (either makes a protein exchange) and a big green salad.

Pineapple-Cucumber Gazpacho (R,V,GF)

Thanks for the recipe, Pat!

> 1 English cucumber
> 1 yellow or orange sweet pepper
> 2 green onions
> ½ large pineapple
> 1 C water
> pinch sea salt

Put everything in a high-powered blender *in the order listed* and blend until it is the consistency you desire, either smooth or a little chunky. Chill or eat at room temperature.

Creamy Cauliflower Soup Too (V,GF)

Thanks for the recipe, Susieq1022

> 2 Tbsp. coconut oil
> 1 Tbsp. extra virgin olive oil
> ½ large onion, coarsely chopped
> 1 garlic clove, minced
> 2 celery stalks, chopped
> 1 large cauliflower, cored and coarsely chopped
> 1 tsp. sea salt
> ½ tsp. thyme
> 1 tsp. dried basil
> 1 tsp. dried marjoram
> 5 C water (up to 1 C more if necessary to cover)
> 1 Tbsp. vegetable bouillon
> *optional*: 6-8 scallions, chopped

In heavy soup kettle, add oil, onion, garlic, and optional scallions. Mix well and cook uncovered over medium heat for several minutes, stirring frequently. Add celery, cauliflower, seasonings, water, and bouillon. Bring to a boil, then reduce heat and simmer covered over medium-low heat for 20 min. or until cauliflower is tender. Remove cover and cool slightly. Pureé in small batches in blender until smooth and creamy, placing blended contents in a second pot. When all is blended, reheat if necessary. *Takes about 35 min. to prepare. Makes 4 servings.*

Lentil Soup (V,GF)

Thanks for the recipe, Tami!

> 1 leek, cleaned and diced
> 2 garlic cloves
> 1 drizzle extra virgin olive oil
> 32 oz. vegetable broth
> 2 carrots, sliced
> 1 C lentils
> 1 C precooked farro
> ⅛ C molasses
> spices of choice (e.g., curry, turmeric, cumin, dried chipotle pepper, paprika,
>   salt, pepper), to taste

Sauté leeks and garlic in olive oil. Add vegetable broth, carrots, and lentils and bring to a boil. Simmer for 20 min. Add farro and desired seasonings. Can be served immediately—but for best results, the flavors come together better the next day. [See Photos section.]

Easy Black Bean Soup (V,GF)

Thanks for the recipe, Tina!

> 2 (15 oz.) cans black beans, drained and rinsed
> 2 C vegetable broth [Use gluten-free broth for GF recipe.]
> 1 C medium salsa
> 1 tsp. ground cumin
> *optional*: sour cream, as garnish [Omit for V recipe.]
> *optional*: fresh chopped cilantro, as garnish

Lightly purée one can of black beans with broth, salsa, and cumin in a blender. In a medium sauce pan, combine puréed bean mixture with remaining beans and heat through. To serve, ladle soup into individual bowls and optionally top each bowl with 1 Tbsp. sour cream and garnish with the chopped cilantro. *Makes 4 servings.*

Stews

Rustic Bean Stew with Kale and Caramelized Onions (V,GF)

Thanks for the recipe, Barbara!

1 Tbsp. coconut oil or extra virgin olive oil

1 lb. yellow onions, sliced ⅛" thick

½ tsp. kosher salt (or to taste)

3 cans black-eyed peas, drained, rinsed, and drained again *OR* 4 C cooked, drained beans (may also use borlotti, small red beans, or Roman beans)

2 bay leaves

2 C vegetable broth

1 Tbsp. balsamic vinegar

1 Tbsp. raw agave

1-2 kale stalks, rinsed, stalk removed, and chopped

freshly ground black pepper, to taste

Preheat pan on medium with coconut or olive oil. Add the onions and toss to coat, then cover and cook until onions are wilted and have released their juices, about 5 min. Uncover, add salt, and sauté until the onions are golden brown, about 20 min. longer. Remove half the onions to a plate and reserve.

To the remaining onions in the pan, add the beans along with the bay leaves, broth, vinegar, and agave. Bring to a simmer, reduce the heat to low, and cook, stirring frequently, until the liquid has reduced considerably and the mixture has a stew-like consistency, about 20 min. During the last 5 min. of cooking, add chopped kale and incorporate. Adjust the seasoning, peppering generously.

Spoon the beans into shallow soup bowls. Top each serving with some of the reserved onions. Great served with crusty whole-grain bread. *Makes 4 servings*.

Lentil & Sweet Potato Stew (V)

Thanks for the recipe, Jode!

> 1 onion, diced
> 3 carrots, chopped
> 3 celery stalks, chopped
> 1 medium sweet potato, peeled and cubed
> 2 garlic cloves, pressed
> ⅓ C pearled barley
> 1 C lentils
> 4 C vegetable broth
> 1 C water (or more, if needed for consistency)
> 1 can diced fire-roasted tomatoes
> 1 C chopped mushrooms
> 1 tsp. cumin
> 1 tsp. rosemary
> 1 tsp. oregano
> 1 bay leaf
> 1 tsp. sea salt

Sauté onion about 5 min. Add carrots and celery and sauté 5 min. more. Add sweet potato, garlic, barley, lentils, broth, and water and simmer 35 min. Add tomatoes, spices, and salt and simmer another 30 min. The stew will be pretty much done at this point, but will get better as it sits.

Spring Stew (V,GF)

Thanks for the recipe, LuAnn!

> 2 ribs celery
> 2 carrots
> 1 round onion OR 4 scallions
> 1 red bell pepper
> 2 medium potatoes
> 4 C milk, any kind (rice, nut, coconut)
> ½ tsp. sea salt
> ⅛ tsp. black pepper
> 1 tsp. dried thyme
> 1 C corn (fresh, if possible)
> 2 Tbsp. cornstarch + ¼ - ½ C water, dissolved and mixed well
> *optional*: ½ lb. crab meat [Omit for V recipe.]

Dice all vegetables into small pieces, put in large soup pot, and sauté in olive oil for 3-5 min. Then add milk, salt, pepper, and thyme and slowly bring to a simmer. Then cover and cook about 15-20 min. until vegetables are tender. Add the corn, optional crab, and cornstarch/water to the pot and stir until bubbly and thickened.

Mexican Stew (V)

Thanks for the recipe, Tami!

(Recipe was adapted by Robyn.)

> 1 drizzle extra virgin olive oil
> 1 small onion, diced
> 1-2 garlic cloves, diced
> 1 can black beans, drained *OR* 1 C dried beans, soaked overnight and drained
> 1 C precooked farro
> 1 can stewed tomatoes, cut into bite-sized pieces
> 1 can tomato sauce *OR* 1 small can V8 juice
> desired spices (dried chipotle pepper, curry, cumin, paprika, salt, pepper, etc.)

Sauté onion and garlic in olive oil. Add remaining ingredients and simmer for 20 min. Serve immediately—or for best results, let rest until cooled, then refrigerate overnight for the flavors to really come together.

Sandwiches

Avocado Tomato Sandwich (V)

Thanks for the recipe, Elizabeth!

> 2 slices sprouted bread
> 1 avocado, sliced
> 1 tomato, sliced
> sea salt, to taste
> 2 Tbsp. balsamic vinegar
> *optional*: 2 Tbsp. flaxseed oil

Toast bread in toaster on highest setting so it's extra crispy. When done, drizzle balsamic vinegar and optional flaxseed oil on each piece. Place avocado slices on bread. Sprinkle with salt. Place tomato slices on top. Sprinkle with salt. Top with other slice of toast. [See Photos section.]

> **Note:** If it's summer, I eat as is. If it's winter, I put the whole sandwich back in my toaster oven and heat a few minutes until the tomato and avocado are warm.

Tabouleh Lettuce Wraps (V,GF)

Thanks for the recipe, Jessica!

> 3 C cooked quinoa (season while cooking, if desired)
> 2 tomatoes, seeds removed and diced small
> 1 cucumber, peeled, seeds removed, and chopped small
> 5 green onions, chopped
> ½ C fresh chopped mint
> ½ C fresh chopped parsley
> juice of 1 lime
> extra virgin olive oil
> sea salt
> freshly ground pepper
> romaine lettuce leaves

Toss quinoa, tomatoes, cucumber, green onions, mint, and parsley in a large bowl to create tabouleh. Spoon mixture into lettuce leaves, squeeze lime juice and drizzle olive oil over top, add salt and pepper to taste, and enjoy!

> **Note:** Lettuce can also be chopped and tossed with other ingredients to make a big salad instead. Substitute soaked bulgur for quinoa for a more traditional tabouleh.

Stores well for up to 3 days in refrigerator.

Mexican Sandwich (V)

Thanks for the recipe, Sean!

> 2 pieces whole-grain bread
> sliced tomato
> guacamole

Spread guacamole on both slices of bread and add tomatoes. Light and awesome!

Tomato Melt

Thanks for the recipe, Sean!

> 2 pieces whole-wheat or whole-grain bread, toasted
> sliced tomato
> goat cheese
> *optional*: spinach

Spread goat cheese on toasted bread, place in nonstick frying pan for a few moments to melt the goat cheese, then add the tomato and optional spinach and top with other piece of toast. [See Photos section.]

Yellow Vegetable Curry (V,GF) (page 32)

Baked Curried Lentils (V,GF) (page 31)

Cado Fajitas (V,GF) (page 36)

Salsa Pizza (GF) (page 7)

Lentil Tacos (V,GF) (page 17)

Lentil Soup (V,GF) (page 69)

Quinoa and Beans and Salsa (V, GF) (page 2)

Southern Red Beans and Rice (V,GF) (page 35)

Zucchini Noodles, Veggies & Spicy Almond Butter Sauce (V,GF) (page 24)

Red, White, & Green Pasta (V,GF) (page 29)

Black Bean Taco Salad (V,GF) (page 116)

Best Raw Burgers Ever (R,V,GF) (page 6)

Anna's Sweet Hash "Partatoes" (V,GF) (page 38)

Pass the Mac and Cheese Please (GF) (page 3)

Quinoa Carrot and Beet Salad (V,GF) (page 118)

Quinoa and Peas (V,GF) (page 32)

Tangy Steamed Kale (V,GF) (page 42)

Buttermilk Dressing (GF) (page 128) on simple salad

Cup of Quinoa Salad (V,GF) (page 116)

Kale and Mango Salad (V,GF) (page 95)

Raw Carrot-Orange Yummy Salad (R,V,GF) (page 110)

Fruit Salad with Honey Lime Mint Dressing (R,V,GF) (page 114)

Minestrone Soup (V,GF) (page 57)

Thai Tomato Soup (V,GF) (page 61)

Tomato Melt (page 75)

Avocado Tomato Sandwich (V) (page 73)

Plain Chia Pudding (R,V,GF) (page 159), chocolate variation

Millet Pudding (GF) (page 158)

Fresh Apple Pie (R,V,GF) (page 144)

Healthy "Sundae" (GF) (page 162)

Raw Key Lime Pie (R,V,GF) (page 142)

Raw Cashew Dream Pie (R,V,GF) (page 141)

Salads & Dressings

Mixed Green Salads

Orange, Radish, and Mint Salad (R,V,GF)

Thanks for the recipe, Barbara!

(Recipe was adapted by Robyn.)

> 4 navel oranges, peeled and chopped
> ½ red onion, thinly sliced
> 8 radishes, halved and thinly sliced
> ¼ C fresh mint leaves, chiffonade
> 2 Tbsp. extra virgin olive oil
> ¼ tsp. sea salt
> freshly ground black pepper, to taste

Toss together the orange sections, onion, radishes, and mint leaves. Drizzle with oil and season with salt and pepper.

Tip: Add the red onion just before serving to avoid a stronger onion flavor.

Kale and Mango Salad (V,GF)

Thanks for the recipe, Brigitte!

> 1 bunch kale (black kale is especially good), stalks removed and discarded, leaves thinly sliced
>
> juice of 1 lemon
>
> ¼ C extra virgin olive oil, plus extra for drizzling
>
> kosher salt
>
> 2 tsp. raw honey
>
> freshly ground black pepper
>
> 1 mango, diced small (about 1 C)
>
> small handful toasted pumpkin seeds (about 2 rounded Tbsp.)

In large serving bowl, add the kale, ½ of lemon juice, a drizzle of oil, and a little kosher salt. Massage until the kale starts to soften and wilt, 2-3 min. Set aside. In a small bowl, whisk remaining lemon juice with the honey and lots of freshly ground black pepper. Stream in the ¼ C oil while whisking until a dressing forms and you like how it tastes. Pour the dressing over the kale and add the mango and pumpkin seeds. Toss and serve. [See Photos section.]

Strawberry Green-Dream Salad (R,V,GF)

Thanks for the recipe, Cynthia (Holistic Nutritionist at www.eatlivefoodstolive.com)!

> ½ C extra virgin olive oil
>
> ¼ C fresh lemon juice
>
> 2 Tbsp. green onion
>
> 1 tsp. grated lemon peel
>
> 2 tsp. dry mustard
>
> 1 tsp. sea salt
>
> 2 Tbsp. raw agave or honey
>
> 1 Tbsp. sesame seeds
>
> spinach and romaine lettuce mix
>
> 3 strawberries (with stems) + additional, for topping
>
> chopped raw almonds, for topping

Blend first eight ingredients until smooth. Pour over spinach/romaine mix. Top with sliced strawberries and chopped almonds.

"Fresh Is In" Salad Plate (R,V,GF)

Thanks for the recipe, Dan Johnson!

> 2 -3 lettuce leaves, chiffonade (stack leaves, roll up into a tight tube, then thinly slice from the end—they will look like confetti on the plate)
>
> 1 medium-sized carrot, cut lengthways into long "julienned" slices, then diced into tiny pieces
>
> 1-2 (depending on size) celery stalks, cut up the same way as the carrots
>
> 2 medium-sized cauliflower bulbs, trimmed down to the smallest-sized bulbs, also dicing the stalks
>
> 4-5 fresh green onions, diced
>
> ¼ C finely diced cucumber
>
> ⅓ C diced apple or pineapple
>
> ¼ C mixture cashews, raisins, and peanuts
>
> 3-4 radishes, diced
>
> ½ tomato, diced

All these ingredients go from the cutting board directly onto the plate. No leftover salad ingredients to go into a bowl in the fridge—fresh is everything!

Vegan Caesar Salad Dressing Recipe—with Hemp Seeds! (R,V,GF)

Thanks for the recipe, Diana!

> romaine lettuce, chopped
>
> 2 -3 whole garlic cloves
>
> 1 tsp. organic Worcestershire
>
> ¼ C fresh lemon juice
>
> ¾ tsp. Dijon mustard
>
> ¼ C extra virgin olive oil
>
> ¼ C organic hemp seeds
>
> sea salt, to taste
>
> freshly ground black pepper, to taste
>
> *optional*: ½ tsp. anchovy paste [Omit for V recipe.]

Place all ingredients except romaine in a blender or food processor and process until smooth and creamy. Pour into serving bowl. Add romaine and toss to coat. *Makes 4 servings*.

Note: Dressing will keep in refrigerator for 3-4 days if stored in a covered container.

Kale Salad (R,V,GF)

Thanks for the recipe, Elizabeth!

> 1 bunch kale (lacinato or dinosaur kale preferred, but curly kale is fine too)
>
> 1 Tbsp. extra virgin olive oil or flaxseed oil
>
> ¼ - ½ tsp. Original Crystal Himalayan or sea salt
>
> 1 avocado
>
> 2 handfuls grape tomatoes, halved lengthwise
>
> 2 scallions, sliced
>
> juice of ½ lemon or lime
>
> *optional*: some chopped olives
>
> *optional*: cayenne, chipotle, or curry powder (to add a kick to the salad)

De-stem kale, then roll leaves up like cigars and chiffonade them. Add them to a bowl with oil and salt, and massage until kale wilts. Add avocado and massage again until kale is coated (leaving some chunks of avocado is fine).

Add, tomatoes, scallions, and optional olives. Add citrus juice and spices and toss. Taste and correct seasonings if needed.

Chef Ellen's Signature Strawberry-Spinach Salad with Poppy-Sesame Dressing (R,V,GF)

Thanks for the recipe, Ellen (www.thewellnessworker.com)!

> 2 lb. baby spinach
> ½ lb. dandelion greens
> 2 C sliced fresh, organic strawberries
> ½ small red onion, thinly sliced
> ½ - ¾ C slivered almonds or walnut pieces
> ½ C walnut oil
> 2-3 Tbsp. balsamic vinegar [Use raw vinegar for R recipe.]
> 1 -2 Tbsp. puréed organic strawberries (fresh or frozen)
> 2 Tbsp. fresh orange juice
> 1 Tbsp. poppy seeds
> 2 Tbsp. sesame seeds
> 2 Tbsp. hemp seeds
> ¼ C raw honey or brown rice syrup [Use brown rice syrup for V recipe.]
> sea salt and black pepper, to taste

In a large bowl, toss together spinach, dandelion greens, strawberries, almonds, red onion. In a medium bowl, whisk together the oil, vinegar, strawberry purée, honey, and orange juice. Pour dressing over the greens mixture and toss to coat. Serve immediately. *Serves 6-8.*

Avocado Lettuce Salad (R,V,GF)

Thanks for the recipe, Gwen!

1 medium ripe avocado, mashed
8 oz. diced tomato
sea salt, to taste
Lemon Dill Dip (Epicure Spices), to taste
Three Onion Dip (Epicure Spices), to taste
8 oz. diced cucumber
8 oz. shredded lettuce

Mix the tomato and avocado together. Then add all dips/spices to taste and mix. Toss the cucumber and lettuce together. Then combine and mix together well.

Pomegranate Citrus Salad (R,V,GF)

Thanks for the recipe, Janelle!

1 pomegranate
1 grapefruit
1 orange
spring mix salad greens
dash stevia

Remove seeds from pomegranate. Peel the grapefruit and oranges, cut up sections if you'd like smaller pieces, and mix with pomegranate seeds. Sprinkle it all with a little stevia. In your presentation bowl, pile up the spring greens, add the fruit mixture, then toss well and serve. *Makes 1-2 servings.*

Orange Poppy Seed Salad with Dressing (R,V,GF)

Thanks for the recipe, Jenna!

>1 head Chinese (Napa) cabbage
>1 head red leaf lettuce
>1 C sliced almonds
>30 oz. mandarin oranges, drained
>½ red onion, thinly sliced

Wash and drain cabbage and lettuce. Cut cabbage leaves in half down the rib, then chop cabbage and lettuce into bite size pieces. Add almonds, oranges, and red onion and toss.

Dressing:

>**Note:** Dressing is only gluten free, not raw or vegan.

>3 Tbsp. raw honey
>1½ Tbsp. poppy seeds
>1 tsp. dry mustard
>1 tsp. sea salt
>1 Tbsp. onion juice
>⅓ C brown rice vinegar
>¾ C extra virgin olive oil

Combine first six dressing ingredients, then add in oil gradually, beating until thick with wire whisk (or make in the blender). Toss salad with dressing and eat immediately. *Makes 8 servings.*

>*Tip:* Don't pour all the dressing directly over all the salad unless it will all get eaten in one sitting. If al of it will not get eaten immediately, serve the desired amount of salad, pour a corresponding amount of dressing on, and mix. Keep leftover salad and dressing separately in fridge.

Basic Green House Salad (V,GF)

Thanks for the recipe, Jessica!

> 1 head romaine lettuce, chopped
> 1 pint grape tomatoes, halved lengthwise
> ½ C slivered almonds, toasted and cooled *OR* ½ C roasted, chopped walnuts
> *optional*: parmesan cheese, to taste [Omit for V recipe.]

Toss all ingredients together and mix well. My favorite dressing to use on this salad is Most Delicious House Dressing (R,V,GF) on page 130.

Field Greens Salad with Dressing (R,V,GF)

Thanks for the recipe, Jody!

> organic field greens of your choice
> 1 apple or pear, sliced
> 1 C fresh raspberries, blueberries, strawberries, or blackberries (or a combination)
> *optional*: chopped pecans and/or crumbled goat cheese [Omit cheese for V recipe.]

Toss all salad ingredients in a bowl.

Dressing:

> 2 Tbsp. extra virgin olive oil
> 2 Tbsp. water
> 1 Tbsp. balsamic vinegar or apple cider vinegar [Use raw vinegar for R recipe.]
> 1 Tbsp. agave nectar
> ¼ - ½ tsp. sea salt

Mix all dressing ingredients together. Drizzle over salad and serve immediately.

Corsican Kale (V,GF)

Thanks for the recipe, Julia Valentine!

(Recipe was adapted by Robyn.)

> 1 bunch dinosaur, curly, or red Russian kale, stems removed
> 2-3 Tbsp. extra virgin olive oil
> 2-3 Tbsp. fresh lemon juice
> ½ - ¾ tsp. Himalayan or other sea salt
> ¼ C pine nuts
> 1 red, yellow, or orange bell pepper, diced
> 2 handfuls grape tomatoes, whole or halved lengthwise
> ½ C pitted kalamata or Greek olives, halved lengthwise
> *optional*: freshly ground black pepper, to taste
> *optional*: crumbled feta cheese, to taste [Omit for V recipe.]

Stack kale leaves and roll tightly, then chiffonade by cutting crosswise into thin strips. Add the lesser amount of olive oil, lemon juice, salt, and optional pepper and massage with hands. Depending on how big your bunch of kale was, you may need to add more salt, lemon juice, and olive oil. Add pine nuts, bell pepper, tomatoes, olives, and optional cheese. Toss and serve. Salad will keep in the fridge about 3 days.

Tip: There is nothing like the taste or texture of pine nuts, but they can be expensive. If you're watching your budget, you can substitute sunflower seeds if you'd like.

Favorite Green Salad with Simple Homemade Dressing (R,V,GF)

Thanks for the recipe, Lisa Gauger!

> 2 large carrots
>
> ⅓ head cabbage (red and green)
>
> ¼ head broccoli crowns
>
> 2 C chopped (washed) spinach
>
> 6-8 C chopped (washed) red leaf lettuce and/or romaine lettuce (or use a premixed bag of lettuces)
>
> 1 red bell pepper
>
> *optional*: tomatoes, cucumbers, celery

Grate carrots into bottom of bowl, thinly slice cabbages, chop broccoli crowns, then mix these together. Add the spinach and lettuce mix, toss well, and store until ready to serve. Before serving, chop up the bell pepper and add. To dress up the salad, optionally add sliced tomatoes, cucumbers, and celery—but wait until just before serving or the juices will cause the lettuce to wilt (store these additions separately and the salad will stay fresh longer).

I really like to presoak sunflower seeds, pumpkin seeds, almonds and chia seeds (loads of protein and other nutritional benefits) and add these items to the bottom of my huge salad dish for my personal lunch, along with homemade salad dressing which follows.

Dressing:

> 1 C organic extra virgin olive oil (first cold pressed, if possible)
>
> ½ C raw, organic apple cider vinegar
>
> ½ C raw, organic Kombucha, gingerade flavor
>
> 2 tsp. oregano
>
> sea salt, to taste

Mix all ingredients in a salad dressing container. You can also add ¼ C fresh lemon or lime juice or also try adding ¼ C coconut aminos to the basic dressing mix. Note that this dressing does separate quickly; shake well before each use.

Summer Salad (R,V,GF)

Thanks for the recipe, Melissa!

> 1 large head romaine, chopped
> 1 tomato, diced
> 1 cucumber, diced
> 1 bunch scallions, chopped
> 1 small bunch parsley, chopped
> 1 handful fresh mint, chopped
> 1-2 garlic cloves, pressed
> sea salt, to taste (1 tsp. or more)
> juice of 1 fresh lemon
> ½ C extra virgin olive oil

Mix all ingredients together and serve. For best results, add oil and lemon juice right before serving. This salad can be served with pita bread. (Dried mint and bottled lemon juice work OK in a pinch.)

Mexican Salsa Salad (R,V,GF)

Thanks for the recipe, Nancy!

> 6 C chopped romaine lettuce
> 1 red pepper, finely diced
> 2 plum tomatoes, finely diced
> ½ avocado, finely diced
> 2 scallions, finely diced
> ½ jalapeño, finely diced (or to taste)
> 1 ear fresh corn, kernels sliced off
> ¼ C finely chopped cilantro

Layer in a bowl *in the order listed.* A Vidalia onion chopper does a great job finely dicing all the veggies. If you eat raw dairy, Monterey Jack is a great addition. *Makes 1 serving.*

Thai Kale Salad (R,GF)

Thanks for the recipe, Odessa!

    1-2 bunches kale, shredded
    4-5 carrots, shredded
    ½ red bell pepper, chopped or diced
    ½ yellow or orange bell pepper, chopped or diced
    ½ cucumber, julienned
    any other veggies, to taste
    ½ C extra virgin olive oil
    3 Tbsp. raw organic peanut butter (creamy, not chunky)
    juice of 1-2 limes
    2 Tbsp. water
    3 small garlic cloves, minced or pressed through garlic press (about 1½ tsp.)
    1-2 tsp. finely grated fresh ginger
    2 Tbsp. raw honey
    1 tsp. cayenne pepper

Toss all greens and veggies together. Separately combine all other ingredients in blender and mix well. Drizzle dressing over salad, top with favorite raw nuts and sprouts, and toss. Enjoy!

Get Up and Go Salad (R,V,GF)

Thanks for the recipe, Robin!

    spinach or romaine lettuce
    avocado
    sprouts
    tomato slices

Combine ingredients in any desired amounts and toss. Dress salad with either flaxseed oil or extra virgin, cold-pressed olive oil, some sea salt, and cracked black pepper.

Kale Salad Too (R,V,GF)

Thanks for the recipe, Tami!

> 1 head kale, thoroughly washed and dried
>
> Garlic Gold Meyer Lemon vinaigrette [If use other vinaigrette, make sure it is raw for R recipe.]
>
> 1 small beet, shredded
>
> 1 carrot, shredded
>
> 1 small jicama, shredded
>
> 10-15 cherry tomatoes, halved
>
> sea salt, to taste
>
> hemp seeds
>
> nutritional yeast

Roll kale leaves and chiffonade them. Place in a large bowl, drizzle with vinaigrette, then massage. Add remaining ingredients, except hemp seeds and nutritional yeast, and toss. Place in bowls and top with hemp seeds and nutritional yeast.

Oriental Cabbage Salad (V,GF)

Thanks for the recipe, Tara!

> ½ head green cabbage, shredded
>
> 4 green onions, chopped
>
> 2 Tbsp. brown rice vinegar
>
> 2 Tbsp. sesame oil or coconut oil, melted
>
> 1-2 tsp. toasted sesame oil
>
> 2 Tbsp. sesame seeds, toasted

Combine cabbage and green onions. Mix together vinegar and oils in a jar and shake vigorously to mix (or use your blender). Pour over cabbage mixture and toss to coat. Just before serving, add sesame seeds and toss again.

Fresh Kale or Collard Greens Salad with Dressing (R,V,GF)

Thanks for the recipe, Teresa!

This salad rocks. I use oranges and just sesame seeds. It seems actually hot from all the garlic. I actually crave this salad.

> 1 head kale or collards green
>
> 8 garlic cloves, minced
>
> 3 citrus (any combination of pink grapefruit, orange, lemon, or lime), peeled and chopped into bite-sized pieces
>
> 1 C chopped almonds
>
> 2 Tbsp. fresh lime or lemon juice
>
> 2 Tbsp. rice vinegar
>
> 3 Tbsp. flaxseed oil
>
> 1-2 Tbsp. tamari or low-sodium soy sauce [Use tamari for GF recipe.]
>
> ¼ - ½ C dried cranberries
>
> ¼ C sesame seeds

Mince garlic and let sit for 15 min. to allow the nutrients to stabilize prior to use. (When the garlic or onions are cut, a cross reaction occurs which stabilizes the micronutrients and allows them to not be lost in cooking or in the marinade.) Chiffonade 1 or 2 kale/collard leaves at a time into thin ¼" - ½" strips. Toss in citrus. Separately mix the flaxseed oil and vinegar or lime juice together and pour over greens and fruit. Let marinate for 1 hr.

Just prior to serving, add soy sauce and toss. Add the chopped almonds, dried cranberries, and sesame seeds. Taste, and if it still seems bitter, add more chopped oranges, tamari, or lime juice to taste.

Dressing:

> 2 Tbsp. rice or balsamic vinegar *OR* 2-3 Tbsp. fresh lemon or lime juice
>
> 3 Tbsp. flaxseed oil
>
> 1-2 Tbsp. tamari or Bragg Liquid Aminos
>
> *optional*: 2-4 Tbsp. sesame seeds or flax seeds
>
> *optional*: 1-2 Tbsp. any nut or seed butter

Mix the oil and vinegar/juice and any optional ingredients and pour over shredded kale and fruit. Let sit for at least 1 hr. Just prior to serving, add soy sauce and toss thoroughly.

Sunshine Salad (R,V,GF)

Thanks for the recipe, Teresa Miller (PHN, Childhood Lead Poisoning Prevention Program)!

> 1 head chopped romaine hearts
> 1 container grape tomatoes
> 1 medium-sized zucchini, diced
> 1 C chopped olives [Use non-heat-treated olives for R recipe.]
> 1 C raw corn kernels (straight off the cob)
> chopped cilantro, to taste
> 2 green onions, chopped
> ½ red bell pepper, diced
> 1 avocado, cubed
> apple cider vinegar, to taste
> extra virgin olive oil, to taste

Toss all together and coat well with the oil and vinegar.

Fruit & Veggie Salads

Marinated Veggie Salad (R,V,GF)

Thanks for the recipe, Amanda!

>red and orange bell peppers, chopped
>red onion, chopped
>broccoli, chopped
>cauliflower, chopped
>carrots, julienned
>½ C extra virgin olive oil
>¼ C balsamic or red wine vinegar [Use raw balsamic for R recipe.]
>1 Tbsp. Dijon mustard
>juice of 1 fresh lemon
>1 garlic clove
>sea salt and black pepper, to taste

Use any amounts of the veggies that you'd like and toss together. Make the vinaigrette by combining all the other ingredients in a blender until combined or whisking well. Toss the salad and vinaigrette together and let sit for a few hours or overnight. It's so easy—make it early in the day and have it for dinner.

Mango and Avocado Salad (R,V,GF)

Thanks for the recipe, Angela!

> 1 Tbsp. balsamic vinegar [Use raw balsamic for R recipe.]
> 1 Tbsp. fresh lime juice
> 2 Tbsp. extra virgin olive oil
> 2 mangos, cubed
> 2 avocados, cubed
> ½ small red onion, diced
> sea salt and freshly ground black pepper, to taste

In a large serving bowl, whisk together vinegar, lime juice, salt, and pepper. Slowly whisk in oil. Toss in mangos, avocado, and red onion and coat well. Serve immediately.

Raw Carrot-Orange Yummy Salad (R,V,GF)

Thanks for the recipe, Barbara!

> 15 medium carrots, peeled and grated
> 7 navel oranges, cubed
> 1½ C raisins
> 1½ C sliced raw almonds
> ⅓ C fresh lemon juice
> ⅓ C virgin coconut oil
> ⅓ C agave
> 1½ tsp. vanilla

Mix and enjoy the sweet taste of a yummy, refreshing salad. [See Photos section.]

Simple Veggie Salad (R,V,GF)

Thanks for the recipe, Candis!

> 1 large avocado, cut up
> 3 small tomatoes, cut up
> 3 oz. mushrooms, cut up
> 1 C sprouts

Combine all ingredients into a bowl. Spray with Bragg Liquid Aminos.

Candy's Lemony Tomato & Cucumber Salad (R,V,GF)

Thanks for the recipe, Candy!

> 2 organic cucumbers, chopped
> 1½ lb. organic grape tomatoes, halved
> ¼ C red onion diced
> ¼ C extra virgin olive oil
> juice of ½ large (or 1 small) lemon
> 1 bunch dill weed, chopped
> sea salt and black pepper, to taste
> *optional*: 1 zucchini, chopped

In a medium-sized salad bowl, combine cucumbers, tomatoes, onions, and optional zucchini. Separately blend together lemon juice and olive oil, then pour over chopped veggies. Add dill, salt, and pepper and mix all together really well. *Makes 4 servings.*

Tangy Potato Salad (V,GF)

Thanks for the recipe, Chelsea G.!

> red potatoes (with skins)
> sauerkraut (homemade or your favorite brand—mine is Bubbies)
> pickles, diced (homemade or your favorite brand—mine is Bubbies)
> extra virgin olive oil
> dried minced onion or fresh green onion, chopped
> sea salt
> black pepper

There are no measurements in this salad. Just wash as many potatoes as you want to get the salad the size you need. Cut up the potatoes into bit-sized pieces. Boil them until tender, then drain and put into a mixing bowl. To the potatoes add some olive oil, pickles, onion, and sauerkraut. At this time I also add in some of the sauerkraut and pickle brine, just to give it more moisture. Add salt and pepper to taste. Tastes great chilled or warm.

Broccoli Woccoli Coleslaw (V,GF)

Thanks for the recipe, Christy!

> 1 pkg. slivered/shaved broccoli
> extra virgin olive oil
> red wine vinegar
> garlic powder
> 1 small can green olives

To broccoli, add olive oil and vinegar to taste and mix. Add olives and garlic powder to taste and mix all together well.

Avocado and Carrot Salad (R,V,GF)

Thanks for the recipe, Hannah-Marie!

> 1 avocado
> 3-5 carrots (more or less to taste)
> handful fresh parsley, celeriac, or coriander (or mix of all three)
> juice of 1 lemon or 2 limes
> 1 Tbsp. Namu Shoyu [Use tamari instead for GF recipe.]
> 1 Tbsp. sesame seeds
> 1 Tbsp. macadamia (or other) nut oil

Food process the first three ingredients. Or you can grate the carrot and hand-chop the other two ingredients for nice presentation. Set salad aside. Mix together the other ingredients with a fork for the dressing, then combine with salad and toss well. *Makes 1 serving.*

Broccoli Salad (R,V,GF)

Thanks for the recipe, Jennifer!

2 bunches raw broccoli, finely chopped

3 Tbsp. red wine vinegar [Use raw vinegar for R recipe.]

1 tsp. sea salt

¼ C extra virgin olive oil

4 garlic cloves

2 tsp. cumin seeds

2 tsp. red pepper flakes

Dissolve the salt in the vinegar, toss with the broccoli, and set aside. Heat the oil until hot but not smoking. Add the garlic, cumin, and red pepper and keep on the heat for 1 min. Pour heated mixture over broccoli, toss to coat, and let it sit for 1 hr.

I like to eat this with some lentils and a small amount of any grain I have in the house. To make it more of a meal, I add some chopped avocado and unhulled sesame seeds or soaked sunflower seeds on top as garnish. Yummy!

Middle Eastern Salad (R,V,GF)

Thanks for the recipe, Jo!

1 C diced fresh tomatoes

1 C diced cucumber

1 C diced red, green, orange, or yellow bell pepper (or combination)

½ C diced purple onion

1 C diced purple cabbage

½ C diced red radish

2 Tbsp. extra virgin olive oil

2 Tbsp. water

2 Tbsp. fresh squeezed lime juice

sea salt and freshly ground pepper, to taste

dried mint leaves (found in the spice section), for garnish

Combine vegetables in a salad bowl and set aside. Separately mix salad dressing ingredients together well, pour over salad, and toss until thoroughly combined. Garnish with dried mint leaves.

Cranberry-Orange Salad (R,V,GF)

Thanks for the recipe, Lori!

> 1 romaine heart
> 8 oz. fresh spinach
> 1 C Craisins
> 2 (11 oz.) cans mandarin oranges
> 1 C coarsely chopped raw walnuts
> 1 C shredded, unsweetened coconut
> 1 batch Maple Syrup Dressing (see Chapter 3 of *12 Steps to Whole Foods* for recipe) or your favorite, slightly sweet dressing [Use raw dressing for R recipe.]

Wash and tear the romaine lettuce into a extra-large bowl and mix together with the spinach. Toss in all remaining ingredients, mix well, and serve immediately.

> *Tip:* If you are taking this salad to a gathering, keep all ingredients separate and toss when ready to serve—or, you can simply set each of the items out and let the people prepare their own (it's what I do).

Fruit Salad with Honey Lime Mint Dressing (R,V,GF)

Thanks for the recipe, Marisa Rogers!

> 8 C fresh fruit salad (your favorite combo or whatever is in season; my favorite combo is sliced fresh strawberries, kiwis, bananas, red seedless grapes, pineapple, and mango)

Honey Lime Mint Dressing:

> *Note:* The dressing is not vegan unless you use agave instead of honey.

> ¼ C fresh lime juice
> ½ C raw honey (more or less to taste)
> 2-3 Tbsp. minced fresh mint leaves (for garnish)
> *optional*: 1 tsp. lime zest

Whisk all ingredients together in bowl or pulse a few times in blender.

Pour over fresh fruit salad and toss. You can also serve the dressing separate and allow people to drizzle the desired amount on their salad. To make a nice presentation, use a melon baller for melons in the fruit salad and garnish with fresh mint sprigs. [See Photos section.]

Raw Pad Thai Salad (R,V,GF)

Thanks for the recipe, Susanne!

2 zucchinis, sliced into strips with a vegetable peeler

2 large handfuls (~2 C) bean sprouts (I also have used sunflower seed sprouts)

¾ C chopped almonds, peanuts, or cashews

1 carrot, sliced into strips

4 green onions, diced

½ C fresh chopped cilantro

juice of 1 lime

1 Tbsp. raw coconut oil

¼ tsp. sea salt

Toss all ingredients together in a bowl until well coated. Add a dash more salt if desired and enjoy!

Pasta, Grain, & Legume Salads

Cup of Quinoa Salad (V,GF)

Thanks for the recipe, Alicia!

> 1 bowl cooked quinoa
> 1 tsp. coconut oil, melted
> ½ - 1 tsp. Bragg Liquid Aminos
> 1 tomato, chopped
> 1 avocado, chopped

Stir all together and enjoy! [See Photos section.]

Black Bean Taco Salad (V,GF)

Thanks for the recipe, Betsy!

> ¾ C canned black beans, rinsed and drained
> 3 C shredded romaine lettuce
> 1 tomato, chopped
> 10 whole-grain tortilla chips, crushed [Use gluten-free chips for GF recipe.]
> ¼ avocado, chopped
> juice of 1 lime
> 1 Tbsp. extra virgin olive oil
> 1 tsp. cumin
> 1 garlic clove, minced
> dash sea salt

Toss beans, vegetables, and chips together. Whisk together lime juice, oil, cumin, garlic and salt into a dressing, then toss everything together and enjoy. [See Photos section.]

Tip: This dressing can also be used to marinate fish before cooking.

Soba Noodle Salad with Miso Vinaigrette (V,GF)

Thanks for the recipe, Evi from Germany!

Salad:

8 oz. soba noodles [Use 100% buckwheat noodles for GF recipe.]

2 carrots, cut into matchsticks

1 head radicchio, thinly sliced

2 green onions, chopped

1½ sheets toasted nori, cut into thin strips

2 Tbsp. toasted sesame seeds

Dressing:

1-2 Tbsp. white miso paste

1 Tbsp. toasted sesame oil

1 Tbsp. rice vinegar

1 tsp. pickled ginger

3 Tbsp. water

Cook soba noodles according to package directions. Rinse under cold water, drain well, and place in large bowl. Add all dressing ingredients into a blender and blend until smooth. Then add dressing mixture into noodles and toss. Combine carrots, radicchio, green onions, nori, and sesame seeds, then toss with noodles. Serve cold.

Quinoa Carrot and Beet Salad (V,GF)

Thanks for the recipe, Gail!

Salad:

    1 C quinoa

    2 C water

    pinch sea salt

    1½ C grated carrot

    1½ C diced apple

    1 C dark raisins

    1 C sliced raw almonds, toasted

    1 C pumpkin seeds, toasted

    1 bunch thinly sliced green onions

    sea salt and freshly ground pepper, to taste

    1½ C grated peeled beets

Vinaigrette:

    ⅓ C extra virgin olive oil

    3 Tbsp. raw apple cider vinegar

    2 Tbsp. lemon juice

    2 Tbsp. Dijon mustard

    2 Tbsp. real maple syrup

    salt and freshly ground black pepper, to taste

Place all vinaigrette ingredients in a jar and shake to combine. Set aside.

Place quinoa in a fine-mesh strainer. Rinse with cold water until water runs clear (this avoids a raw or bitter taste). Place in medium saucepan, add water, and bring to a boil on high heat. Reduce heat to medium-low and simmer partially covered for 10 to 15 min. or until all the water is absorbed. Fluff quinoa with a fork, then rinse under cold water using a fine mesh strainer and drain well.

Combine cooled quinoa with all other salad ingredients except beets in a large bowl. Drizzle salad with vinaigrette and toss gently to combine. Add beets and gently toss. *Makes 6 servings.* [See Photos section.]

Warm Quinoa & Vegetable Salad (V,GF)

Thanks for the recipe, Heidi!

1 C quinoa

2 C vegetable broth or water

1 Tbsp. dried thyme

1 Tbsp. dried parsley

2 garlic cloves, minced *OR* 1 Tbsp. dried garlic

2 C peas (fresh or frozen)

2 Tbsp. coconut oil

1 small onion, chopped

2-3 large carrots, chopped

2-3 celery stalks, chopped

1 fennel bulb, chopped

4-5 mushrooms, chopped

½ red pepper, chopped

1-2 zucchini, chopped

sea salt and black pepper, to taste

Cook quinoa in broth with spices (thyme, basil, parsley, garlic) in a medium saucepan until boiling, then turn heat to low and simmer for 10 min. Set aside and fold in peas. In a large cast iron frying pan sauté onion, carrots, celery, peppers, fennel, mushrooms, and zucchini (and any other vegetables, if desired) in coconut oil for a few minutes until lightly browned. Put quinoa/peas in a large bowl, mix in sautéed vegetables, then add salt and pepper. Eat alone or serve with a green salad.

Quinoa Salad (V,GF)

Thanks for the recipe, Helen!

(Recipe was adapted by Robyn.)

> 1 C quinoa, cooked according to package directions*
> carrots (amount to taste)
> tomatoes (amount to taste)
> cucumbers (amount to taste)
> celery (amount to taste)
> 1 small red onion
> 3-4 garlic cloves
> 1-2 bunches cilantro, chopped
> 1 bunch parsley, chopped

I soak quinoa in water for 8+ hours and cook with only 1 C broth or water. A rice cooker works best for me.

Finely chop all veggies by hand or use food processor (I process each item separately so nothing turns to mush).

Mix everything together in a large bowl, then add some frozen corn, black beans, and anything else you like in pasta salad and drizzle with extra virgin olive oil (I use red palm oil, but not everyone has that in their pantry) and some fresh lemon juice. Lastly, salt and pepper to taste.

I make a huge batch of this every week and eat it just as is—or spoon it onto a bed of lettuce with salsa or dressing.

Sesame Soba Salad (V,GF)

Thanks for the recipe, Janette!

(Recipe was adapted by Robyn.)

Salad:

> 2 C chopped Napa cabbage
>
> 1 C chopped red cabbage
>
> ½ C julienned carrot
>
> ½ C julienned red pepper
>
> ½ C julienned cucumber
>
> ¼ C chopped scallions
>
> ½ C chopped cilantro
>
> 1 pkg. soba noodles, cooked according to package directions, drained, and rinsed [Use 100% buckwheat noodles for GF recipe.]

Toss together all ingredients for the salad.

Dressing:

> ⅓ C fresh lime juice
>
> ⅓ C Nama Shoyu [Use tamari instead for GF recipe.]
>
> 2 Tbsp. sesame oil
>
> 2 Tbsp. raw honey, agave or maple crystals, to taste [Use agave or maple crystals for V recipe.]
>
> 1 Tbsp. diced jalapeno
>
> 1 Tbsp. grated ginger
>
> 3 garlic cloves

Blend dressing ingredients until smooth. Add desired amount to salad and toss well. Serve immediately or refrigerate.

Mediterranean Quinoa Salad (GF)

Thanks for the recipe, Kate!

(Recipe was adapted by Robyn.)

> 2 C water
>
> equivalent of 2 cubes Better Than Bouillon
>
> 1 garlic clove, smashed (but not broken up)
>
> 1 C uncooked quinoa
>
> 1 pkg. seitan or tempeh [Use gluten-free tempeh for GF recipe.]
>
> 1 large red onion, diced
>
> 1 large green bell pepper, diced
>
> ½ C chopped kalamata olives
>
> ½ C crumbled feta cheese
>
> ¼ C chopped fresh parsley
>
> ¼ C chopped fresh chives
>
> 1 tsp. sea salt
>
> ⅔ C fresh lemon juice
>
> 1 Tbsp. balsamic vinegar
>
> ¼ C extra virgin olive oil

Bring the water, Better Than Bouillon, and garlic to a boil in a saucepan. Stir in the quinoa, then reduce heat to medium-low, cover, and simmer until the quinoa is tender and the water has been absorbed, 15 to 20 min. Discard the garlic clove and scrape the quinoa into a large bowl. Gently stir the seitan/tempeh, onion, pepper, olives, feta cheese, parsley, chives, and salt into the quinoa. Drizzle in the lemon juice, balsamic vinegar, and olive oil. Stir until evenly mixed. Serve warm or refrigerate and serve cold. *Makes 8 servings.*

Lentil Salad (V,GF)

Thanks for the recipe, Kathy!

> 1 (16 oz.) pkg. organic green or black lentils, cooked until just firm and cooled
>
> 2 C cooked organic brown rice, cooled
>
> 1 organic onion, coarsely chopped
>
> 1 organic red bell pepper, coarsely chopped
>
> 3 large organic carrots, peeled and coarsely chopped
>
> 1 C marinated artichoke hearts, drained
>
> ⅓ C capers, drained
>
> 1 can black olives, drained
>
> vinegar of choice, to taste (I do not recommend using balsamic unless it's white balsamic due to the dark color of it, which makes the salad look rather muddy)
>
> sea salt, to taste
>
> freshly ground pepper, to taste

While the lentils and rice are cooling, place the onion in a food processor and pulse until it is chopped into small pieces but not puréed. Then do the same with the red pepper, carrots, artichoke hearts, and olives so that everything is sort of uniform in size relative to the size of the lentils. Put veggies in a large bowl with the cooled rice and lentils, then add capers, vinegar, salt, and pepper and gently fold the mixture so as to keep the lentils intact. Adjust seasonings if needed. Salad will keep at least 5 days in your refrigerator.

Blueberry Pasta Salad (V)

Thanks for the recipe, Linda!

> 1 large vidalia onion, finely chopped
> 1 tsp. coconut oil (if sautéing)
> 2 celery stalks, finely chopped
> 2 C French cut or whole string beans
> 1 C blueberries, divided (fresh or frozen)
> ½ C spinach (fresh or frozen)
> ¼ C balsamic vinegar (or to taste)
> freshly ground black pepper, to taste
> 1 box organic whole-wheat pasta
> *optional*: 1 tsp. raw honey or agave, if need some sweetness [Use agave for V recipe.]

While the water is boiling for the pasta, sauté the onion, then toss the celery, beans, spinach, and ¼ C of the blueberries together in the pan. Allow for thawing if berries are frozen, then gently mash the blueberries to render their juice. Splash in the balsamic vinegar and grate some black pepper, then let it sit off the heat while the pasta completes cooking. If the vinegar is a little too tart for your (or your young ones') taste, add the optional agave/honey to cut the tartness. Once pasta is cooked, stir it into the sautéd mixture. Serve with a nice salad and you are good to go!

This dish can be served with the vegetables raw or lightly sautéed in coconut oil. And if you are in a big hurry or fresh is not available, you can use frozen vegetables and blueberries.

> *Tip:* If you are not opposed to dairy or egg, you could make this a creamier version by stirring in a small amount of plain organic or Greek yogurt or mayonnaise—but it is very good without.

Fresh Mediterranean Veggie Bulgur Salad (V)

Thanks for the recipe, Patrice!

1 C bulgur

1½ C boiling water

1½ tsp. Organic Better Than Bouillon veggie base (from Costco)

1 orange bell pepper, seeded and chopped (or any combination of colors)

½ C finely chopped parsley

1 C sliced carrots

1 C finely chopped cauliflower florets (cut floret pieces ½" long, but thinly slice and then chop the stem part)

1 C finely chopped broccoli florets (cut floret pieces ½" long, but thinly slice and then chop the stem part)

¼ C chopped green or red onion

⅛ C sliced kalamata ore regular black olives

1 C grape tomatoes, sliced in half or thirds

1 C julienned snow peas or sugar snap peas

1 C petite green peas

½ C artichoke hearts, cut to any size you like

1 Tbsp. fresh lemon juice

garlic, to taste

black pepper, to taste

sea salt, to taste

optional: 2 Tbsp. extra virgin olive oil, if salad is dry

Add bulgur and veggie base to the boiling water. Cover and reduce heat to simmer for 20 min. Bulgur should absorb the water and be somewhat dry. Set aside to cool.

Combine all the other ingredients together well, then add to the cooled bulgur and toss. Add ⅓ C crumbled or small-cubed feta cheese and folded in just before serving. Refrigerate. Serve with a side of sliced avocado, hummus, and warmed pita bread.

Note: The idea of this salad is that you can add whatever are your favorite veggies or whatever you have in your fridge. You can also add grilled chicken tenders that have been seasoned to taste and then cut into bite-sized pieces—though, to me, it is great meatless.

Veggie-Explosion Quinoa Salad (V)

Thanks for the recipe, Tina!

    4-6 C cooked quinoa
    2 Roma tomatoes, diced
    ½ green bell pepper, chopped
    ½ red bell pepper, chopped
    1 carrot, diced
    1 celery stalk, diced
    1 green onion, chopped
    handful raw mushrooms, chopped
    ½ C raw cashews
    ½ - ¾ C Cabbage Salad Dressing (from Ch. 3 of *12 Steps to Whole Foods*)
    optional: Parmesan cheese [Omit for V recipe.]

Combine cooked quinoa (either hot or cooled), nuts, and veggies. Toss well with Cabbage Salad Dressing. Top with a little Parmesan cheese if desired.

Dressings

Vinaigrette Dressing (R,V,GF)

Thanks for the recipe, Amanda!

½ C extra virgin olive oil
¼ C balsamic or red wine vinegar [Use raw vinegar for R recipe.]
1 Tbsp. Dijon mustard
juice of 1 fresh lemon
1 garlic clove
sea salt and black pepper, to taste

Blend or whisk until well combined. (See used in Marinated Veggie Salad (R,V,GF) on page 109.)

Taco Salad Dressing (R,V,GF)

Thanks for the recipe, Betsy!

juice of 1 lime
1 Tbsp. extra virgin olive oil
1 tsp. cumin
1 garlic clove, minced
dash sea salt

Whisk all together well. (See used in Black Bean Taco Salad (V,GF) on page 116.) *Makes 1 serving.*

Tip: The dressing can also be used to marinate fish before cooking.

Parsley-Cucumber Dressing (R,V,GF)

Thanks for the recipe, Debra!

½ English cucumber
⅓ C soaked raw almonds
1 clove garlic
¼ C fresh parsley
1/3 C Udo's oil (or any healthy oil)
½ tsp. sea salt

Blend all ingredients together in a high speed blender. I especially like to use this dressing on broccoli-cauliflower salad.

Buttermilk Dressing (GF)

Thanks for the recipe, Delia!

2 C Vegannaise
1½ C buttermilk
2 Tbsp. raw white wine vinegar or rice vinegar
½ C chopped fresh green onions or chives
1 tsp. raw agave
sea salt and black pepper, to taste

Whisk all ingredients together until smooth and well combined. Chill. [See Photos section.]

Miso Vinaigrette (R,V,GF)

Thanks for the recipe, Evi from Germany!

1-2 Tbsp. white miso paste
1 Tbsp. toasted sesame oil
1 Tbsp. rice vinegar
1 tsp. pickled ginger
3 Tbsp. water

Add all to blender and mix until smooth. (See used in Soba Noodle Salad with Miso Vinaigrette (V,GF) on page 117.)

Sesame Dressing (V,GF)

Thanks for the recipe, Janette!

(Recipe was adapted by Robyn.)

⅓ C fresh lime juice

⅓ C Nama Shoyu [Use tamari instead for GF recipe.]

2 Tbsp. sesame oil

2 Tbsp. raw honey, agave or maple crystals, to taste [Use agave or maple crystals for V recipe.]

1 Tbsp. diced jalapeno

1 Tbsp. grated ginger

3 garlic cloves

Blend dressing ingredients until smooth. (See used in Sesame Soba Salad (V,GF) on page 121.)

Orange Poppy Seed Dressing (R,GF)

Thanks for the recipe, Jenna Strawn!

3 Tbsp. raw honey

1½ Tbsp. poppy seeds

1 tsp. dry mustard

1 tsp. sea salt

1 Tbsp. onion juice

⅓ C brown rice vinegar [Use raw vinegar for R recipe.]

¾ C extra virgin olive oil

Combine first six dressing ingredients, then add in oil gradually, beating until thick with wire whisk (or make in the blender). (See used in Orange Poppy Seed Salad with Dressing (R,V,GF) on page 100.)

Most Delicious House Dressing (R,V,GF)

Thanks for the recipe, Jessica!

juice of 1 lemon
⅔ C extra virgin olive oil
4 garlic cloves, crushed
1 tsp. sea salt
½ tsp. fresh ground pepper

Shake everything very well in jar. If you refrigerate this dressing, it will harden and before using, you will need to let it warm up to room temp and shake again! Use this with a yummy green salad, such as my Basic Green House Salad (V,GF) on page 101.

Maple Vinaigrette Dressing (V,GF)

Thanks for the recipe, Kathy!

1 tsp. dry mustard
½ tsp. dried basil
¼ C balsamic, wine, or cider vinegar
½ C pure maple syrup
1 Tbsp. fresh lemon juice
1 clove garlic, minced
1 C extra-virgin olive oil
1 tsp. sea salt
¼ tsp. ground pepper

Combine mustard and basil in a small bowl. Whisk in vinegar, maple syrup, lemon juice, and garlic. Add olive oil and continue whisking until ingredients are well combined. Season with salt and pepper. Refrigerated, the dressing will keep for several weeks.

Simple Homemade Salad Dressing (R,V,GF)

Thanks for the recipe, Lisa Gauger!

> 1 C organic extra virgin olive oil (first cold pressed, if possible)
> ½ C raw, organic apple cider vinegar
> ½ C raw, organic Kombucha, gingerade flavor
> 2 tsp. oregano
> sea salt, to taste

Mix all ingredients in a salad dressing container. You can also add ¼ C fresh lemon or lime juice or also try adding ¼ C coconut aminos to the basic dressing mix. Note that this dressing does separate quickly; shake well before each use. (See used in my Favorite Green Salad with Simple Homemade Dressing (R,V,GF) on page 103.)

Honey Lime Mint Dressing (R,V,GF)

Thanks for the recipe, Marisa Rogers!

> ¼ C fresh lime juice
> ½ C raw honey (more or less to taste) [Use agave instead to make V recipe.]
> 2-3 Tbsp. minced fresh mint leaves (for garnish)
> *optional*: 1 tsp. lime zest

Whisk all ingredients together in bowl or pulse a few times in blender. (See used in Fruit Salad with Honey Lime Mint Dressing (R,V,GF) on page 114.)

Thai Salad Dressing (R,GF)

Thanks for the recipe, Odessa!

> ½ C extra virgin olive oil
> 3 Tbsp. raw organic peanut butter (creamy, not chunky)
> juice of 1-2 limes
> 2 Tbsp. water
> 3 small garlic cloves, minced or pressed through garlic press (about 1½ tsp.)
> 1-2 tsp. finely grated fresh ginger
> 2 Tbsp. raw honey
> 1 tsp. cayenne pepper

Blend all in a blender until smooth. (See used with Thai Kale Salad (R,GF) on page 105.)

Japanese Ginger Salad Dressing (R,V,GF)

Thanks for the recipe, Sarah!

> ¼ C tamari
> juice of ½ lemon
> 3 Tbsp. minced fresh ginger root
> 2 tsp. raw agave
> ½ C raw rice vinegar
> 1 tsp. tahini
> pinch Himalayan or other sea salt
> *optional*: 3 garlic cloves, minced
> *optional*: 1 tsp. prepared Dijon-style mustard

Mix all ingredients until smooth.

Coleslaw Dressing (GF)

Thanks for the recipe, Wayne Green (www.waynegreen.com)

> 1 qt. organic plain yogurt
> 1 C organic, raw apple cider vinegar
> 1 C extra virgin olive oil
> ½ C raw honey
> 2 Tbsp. celery seed
> 1 Tbsp. sea salt
> 1 Tbsp. cracked pepper

Put all in your blender and mix thoroughly.

This is a coleslaw sauce that can be added to any minced vegetable to add a sweet-sour-creamy flavor. Blending a generous helping of the sauce and tomatoes makes a fabulous raw tomato soup. I mince carrots, yams, asparagus, broccoli, snow peas, red cabbage, cauliflower, etc., and stir in some sauce with each.

Desserts

Pies, Cakes, & Frostings

PIES

Chocolate Tofu Pie (V)

Thanks for the recipe, Alina!

(Recipe was adapted by Robyn.)

Crust:

> ¾ C whole-wheat flour
> ¾ C ground almonds
> 1 tsp. Sucanat or coconut palm sugar
> 10 Tbsp. Smart Balance margarine (vegan version)

Preheat oven to 325°. Mix the flour, almonds, and Sucanat/sugar with the margarine to form a crust. Coat an 8" round baking pan with additional margarine and press the crust into it. Bake for about 10 min.

Filling:

> 1½ lb. firm tofu
> 1¼ C Sucanat or coconut palm sugar
> ¾ C cold-pressed extra virgin coconut or olive oil
> ½ C fresh orange juice
> 2 Tbsp. cacao
> 2-3 tsp. almond essence

Blend all ingredients together, pour into the crust, and bake for 75 min. Best served after it is refrigerated for a day.

Lemon Curd Pie (R,V,GF)

Thanks for the recipe, Barbara (www.eatrawfeelgreat.co.uk)!

Crust:

> ½ C blanched almonds, soaked
> 1 Tbsp. sesame oil
> ½ C hulled sesame seeds
> ¼ C white almond butter
> 8 drops stevia *OR* 1 Tbsp. raw agave or honey
> pinch sea salt
> zest of 2 lemons (~ 1 Tbsp.)

Combine all ingredients in the food processor until they come together. Press into the bottom and sides of a 7" tart pan with a removable bottom. Put in fridge to set.

Filling:

> juice of 4 lemons (~ ½ C)
> zest of 2 lemons (~ 1 Tbsp.)
> ½ C cocoa butter
> ½ C coconut oil
> ¼ C white almond butter
> 8 drops of stevia *OR* 3 Tbsp. raw agave or honey
> *optional*: lemon zest/blueberries/pomegranate seeds/borage flowers, for
>   garnish

Put the cocoa butter and coconut oil in a tall glass and partially submerge in a larger glass or a bowl of hot water to melt. Then combine with the rest of the ingredients in the food processor and blend until smooth. Taste for sweetness and adjust if necessary, taking into account that the sharpness of the lemon will diminish in the fridge. Add filling to the crust. Smooth the top and leave in fridge for at least 2 hr. to set. Decorate with garnish if desired. Pie will keep in the fridge for 1-2 days or can be frozen.

My Favorite Is Key Lime Pie (R,V,GF)

Thanks for the recipe, Beverly Watson!

Crust:

> 1 C raw walnuts or pecans, soaked and dried
> 1 C unsweetened shredded dried coconut
> ¼ tsp. sea salt
> 6 Medjool dates, pitted and soaked

Process all together and press into pie plate. Keep a few crumbs for the topping.

Filling:

> ¾ C fresh lime juice
> ½ - ¾ C raw agave
> ¼ tsp. sea salt
> 2 C mashed avocado
> ½ C melted coconut oil
> 1 Tbsp. psyllium powder

Blend all in blender. Then pour into crust, sprinkle with reserved crust crumbs, and cool for 2 hr. Keeps very well in the fridge for 5-6 days.

Berry Cobbler (R,GF)

Thanks for the recipe, Deanna!

Crust:

      ½ C almonds
      ½ C walnuts
      2 pinches sea salt
      dash extra virgin olive oil
      4-5 dates, pitted
      2 Tbsp. raw honey

Blend everything together well. Firmly pack the mixture into the bottom of a 9"x13" baking dish, then set it aside to make the filling.

Filling:

      2 C red raspberries, divided
      2 C blackberries, divided
      pinch sea salt
      2-3 dates, pitted
      2 Tbsp. raw honey
      dash fresh lemon juice

Put all except ½ C raspberries and ½ C blackberries into a food processor. Mix well, then put into large bowl. Lightly mix the 1 C of reserved berries together so they are chunky. Then add to the bowl and incorporate everything together. Pour the filling into the crust and garnish the top with some additional whole fresh raspberries and blackberries.

Grandma's Chocolate Zucchini Cake (GF)

Thanks for the recipe, Desirée Hancock (www.unconventionalkitchen.com)!

1 C Sucanat

½ C coconut oil or butter

3 eggs (organic, free range)

⅓ C mashed banana

2 tsp. vanilla

¾ C agave

¾ C buttermilk*

2¼ C kamut flour (oat, white whole-wheat flour)

1 tsp. cinnamon

½ tsp. salt

1 tsp. baking powder

1 tsp. baking soda

4 Tbsp. cocoa powder

½ C chopped walnuts

½ C dark chocolate chips (from health food store, naturally sweetened)

* To make sour milk with almond milk, just add a scant tablespoon of vinegar to the almond milk and let it sit for 5 min. while you prepare your other ingredients.

Preheat oven to 350°. Grease a glass 9"x13" baking dish. In a large mixing bowl, beat the Sucanat and butter/coconut oil together until creamy. Add the eggs one at a time and beat to incorporate. Next add the agave, buttermilk, mashed banana, and vanilla and mix well. In a separate bowl, whisk together the dry ingredients: flour, cinnamon, salt, baking soda, baking powder, and cocoa powder.

Stir the dry ingredients into the wet ingredients, being careful not to overmix. Fold in the chocolate chips and walnuts to the batter. Pour the batter into the baking dish and bake for 35 min. *Makes 1 cake (about 12-15 servings).*

Yummy Squash Pie (R,V,GF)

Thanks for the recipe, Fern!

Crust:

> 1-2 C almonds, soaked
>
> 3-4 tsp. real maple syrup

Soak almonds 8-12 hr., drain, rinse, and drain again. Dry the nuts off with a towel, then put them in the sun to thoroughly dry (or use dehydrator). Process the almonds until uniformly very fine. Gradually add the maple syrup, only enough until the almond meal holds together. Sprinkle and then gently press the crust into the bottom and sides of a pie plate.

Filling:

> 2 C shredded winter squash, seeds, inner "strings," and rind removed
>
> 1 C soaked dates
>
> 2 tsp. cinnamon
>
> 1 tsp. freshly diced ginger
>
> 1 tsp. nutmeg
>
> 1 tsp. coconut oil
>
> dash vanilla
>
> ¼ C water

Process raw/uncooked squash "flesh" in blender, then add the rest of the ingredients and blend until smooth. You might need to add more liquid to get it to blend well. Pour into crust and chill in the refrigerator for at least 30 min. before serving. This yummy squash pie can rival even the most traditional of pumpkin pies.

Home Style Blueberry Cobbler (V)

Thanks for the recipe, Garon!

(Recipe was adapted by Robyn.)

> 1 C whole-wheat pastry flour
> 1 C (scant) coconut palm sugar or Sucanat
> 1 C vanilla or plain almond milk
> 1 Tbsp. fresh lemon juice
> ¼ C Earth Balance "margarine," melted
> 1 tsp. aluminum-free baking powder
> 1 tsp. sea salt
> 1 C berries, any kind (fresh or frozen)

Preheat the oven to 350° and grease a 9" glass pie plate. Put the lemon juice in a measuring cup, and pour in the almond milk till it reaches the 1 C mark. Set aside for at least 5 min.—this will make "buttermilk."

Meanwhile, combine the flour, sugar, baking powder, and salt in a large bowl and whisk together. Pour the "buttermilk" and the melted Earth Balance into the bowl with the flour mixture. Using a spatula (not the whisk), gently mix everything together until just combined. There will probably be lumps, which is OK.

Pour the batter into the greased pie plate and add the berries to the batter. Bake for 45 min., or until a toothpick comes out clean. Allow to cool at least 10-15 min.

The blueberries will have burst during baking and permeated the cake with their juicy goodness. The cakey part is light, fluffy, and über-moist. *Yields 8-10 slices.*

Raw Cashew Dream Pie (R,V,GF)

Thanks for the recipe, Kandace!

Crust:

>½ C raw almonds, pecans, or walnuts (not soaked)
>
>½ C soft Medjool dates
>
>¼ tsp. sea salt

Place nuts, dates, and salt in a food processor and pulse to chop until desired consistency. Scoop mixture into bottom of baking dish. (You may use a spring-form pan if you want a beautiful presentation.) Press crust firmly.

Filling:

>1½ C raw cashews, soaked for at least 5 hr. (overnight is best)
>
>juice of 2 lemons
>
>seeds of 1 vanilla bean *OR* 1 tsp. alcohol-free vanilla extract
>
>⅓ C raw coconut oil, melted
>
>⅓ C raw honey (solid or liquid) or agave nectar [Use agave for V recipe.]
>
>1 C raspberries

Warm coconut oil and honey/agave in a small saucepan on low heat until liquefied and whisk to combine. Using a high-powered blender, blend all ingredients except raspberries. Pour ⅔ of the mixture into the crust. Then add raspberries to the remaining filling, mix together, and pour on top of pie. Freeze until ready to serve. Remove from freezer shortly before serving to defrost a little. [See Photos section.]

>**Tip:** This can be made in a variety of flavors other than raspberry. I really like chocolate—I simply substitute about ¼ C raw cocoa powder and 1 Tbsp. agave for the raspberries. Very rich and delicious.

Raw Key Lime Pie (R,V,GF)

Thanks for the recipe, Kelly!

Crust:

> 1 C pecans
> 1 C walnuts
> 6 Medjool dates, pitted
> ¼ tsp. nutmeg
> ¼ tsp. cinnamon
> dash sea salt

In a food processor or blender, mix to desired texture. Transfer to 8"x12" glass dish or 10" pie plate and press evenly to sides and bottom.

Filling:

> 9-10 ripe avocados
> 1¼ C lime juice
> 1¼ C raw agave

Combine in food processor with S blade, blending until very smooth. Pour into crust and garnish as desired. *Serves 12.* [See Photos section.]

> *Tip:* I also make this filling regularly for breakfast or a snack, using many kinds of fruit in place of the limes for variety: strawberry, banana, lemon, blueberry, raspberry, etc. I reduce the recipe to one-tenth for a single serving.

Raw Coconut Chocolate Mousse Pie (R,V,GF)

Thanks for the recipe, Michael!

Crust:

> 1½ C shredded coconut
> 1 C raw walnuts (not soaked)
> ½ C pecans
> 1 Tbsp. raw agave
> ¾ C pitted, chopped Medjool dates (not soaked)
> dash pink Himalayan unrefined sea salt

Combine all in processor with S blade until it achieves the consistency of a crust. Press into 9" pie plate.

Filling:

> 1¾ C raw cashews (not soaked)
> ¾" piece vanilla bean
> 1 Tbsp. organic cacao chocolate powder (Sunfood - Nutrition)
> 1 Tbsp. golden ground flax seeds
> dash Pink Himalayan unrefined sea salt
> 1 young coconut
> 6-8 ice cubes
> cacao nibs or sliced strawberries or kiwis

Combine cashews, vanilla bean, cacao powder, flax seeds, and salt in blender. Pulse several times. Drain liquid from coconut into blender, then scrape coconut meat into blender as well. Add ice and blend until smooth and creamy. Top with cacao nibs or sliced strawberries or kiwis. Chill in refrigerator for 4-6 hr. until set.

Fresh Apple Pie (R,V,GF)

Thanks for the recipe, Robina!

I serve this pie frequently to guests and take it to parties and potlucks. No one ever guesses it is raw—they just think that it is a particularly delicious apple pie. But I never seem to be able to bring any back home with me, darn....

Crust:

> 2 C raw almonds, sprouted and dehydrated if you have them—otherwise, just dry almonds
>
> 1 tsp. unrefined salt (Real, Himalayan, Hawaiian)
>
> 1 C pitted dates

In a Cuisinart (or other food processor) with an S blade and a 1 or 2 mm slicing blade, process the almonds and salt together until almonds are an average size of a large quinoa seed or GrapeNut (some of the almond bits will be bigger and some smaller—you want them to still be crunchy). Slowly add and process the dates with the almonds/salt until they form a dough. Press dough into the bottom and up the sides of a medium-deep pie dish to form the crust. Set aside.

Filling:

> 5 or 6 organic apples (my favorite is Fuji because it is reliably crisp, but any variety is great)
>
> 1 C dried fruit (goji, raisins, mulberry, etc.—use your imagination!)
>
> 2 Tbsp. cinnamon (yes, that is 2 Tbsp.—if it is a really strong cinnamon, use 1½ Tbsp.)
>
> 1 orange, peeled and seeded
>
> ½ C pitted dates
>
> water, as needed for consistency

Slice the apples very thin or run them through the processor slicer disc. Then toss the apples, dried fruit, and cinnamon in a very large bowl until everything is coated pretty evenly with the cinnamon.

Add first the oranges and then the dates in the high-powered blender and blend, adding teaspoons of water until the mixture forms a medium-consistency syrup. Add the syrup to the apples/dried fruit and mix together well. Spoon the filling into the pie dish and round off the top. If not eaten immediately, store in fridge.

We all think this pie tastes wonderful the next day or even the day after that—the flavors keep blending and softening. [See Photos section.]

Blender Quinoa Chocolate Cake (GF)

Thanks for the recipe, Aimee (www.aimeehenrikson.blogspot.com)!

⅔ C white or golden quinoa, uncooked

1⅓ C water

⅓ C creamy nut milk (almond or cashew)

4 large eggs (organic, free range)

1 tsp. vanilla extract

¾ C coconut oil, melted

1½ C coconut palm sugar or Sucanat

1 C unsweetened cocoa powder

1½ tsp. baking powder, aluminum free

½ tsp. baking soda

½ tsp. sea salt

Preheat oven to 350°. Combine the water and the quinoa in a medium saucepan and bring to a boil. Reduce heat, cover, and simmer for 10 min. Fluff with a fork and cool. You can also use leftover quinoa with great results.

Lightly grease two 8" round cake pans (or one large square pan). Line the bottoms of the pans with parchment paper. Combine almond milk, eggs, and vanilla in a high-powered blender and pulse to incorporate. Then add the quinoa and coconut oil and blend until smooth.

Whisk together sugar, cocoa powder, baking powder, and baking soda in a medium bowl. Add the contents of the blender and mix well. Divide the batter between the two pans and bake on center rack of oven for 40-45 min. (until a knife inserted comes out clean). Remove cakes from oven and cool completely in the pans before serving.

Tip: You can frost either cake, or you could even make a two-layer cake using the Coconut Chocolate Ganache (V,GF) (page 147) or Yummy Chocolate Frosting (V,GF) (page 148), pecans, walnuts, slivered almonds, and/or berries (strawberries or raspberries), and Whipped Coconut Cream (R,V,GF) (page 34).

Blueberry-Flaxseed Upside-Down Cakes

Thanks for the recipe, Leah!

(Recipe was adapted by Robyn.)

> 6 Tbsp. melted butter
> ¾ C whole-wheat flour
> ⅓ C flax seeds
> 1 tsp. aluminum-free baking powder
> ¼ tsp. sea salt
> ⅓ egg (organic, free range) *OR* 1 tsp. chia soaked in 1 Tbsp. water for 10 min.
> 1 C almond or rice milk
> ½ C coconut palm sugar or Sucanat
> ¾ C blueberries (fresh or frozen)

Preheat oven to 350°. Using 2 Tbsp. of the melted butter, grease 10 muffin tins. Combine flour, seeds, baking powder, and salt in small bowl. Wisk together remaining melted butter, egg, milk, and sugar in large bowl. Add dry mixture and whisk until smooth. Pour into muffin tins and add blueberries on top. Bake 20 min., then store wrapped in parchment paper.

Almond Berry Cake (R,V,GF)

Thanks for the recipe, Tammy!

> 2 C shredded raw carrots
> 2 C almonds, finely chopped
> 12-15 dates, finely chopped
> 3-4 bananas, sliced
> unsweetened shredded coconut
> fresh or frozen berries (any kind)
> Coconut-Cashew Frosting (R,V,GF) (page 147)

In a large bowl, mix carrots, almonds, and dates together. Sprinkle coconut in the bottom of an 8"x8" glass pan and press ½ of the carrot mixture into pan. Place banana slices on top of mixture.

Spread ½ of the frosting over the bananas. Lightly press the remaining carrot mixture over frosting, then spread the remaining frosting on top.

Blend berries and spread on top of cake. Garnish with more whole berries. Refrigerate for several hours before serving.

FROSTINGS

Coconut-Cashew Frosting (R,V,GF)

Thanks for the recipe, Tammy!

      1 C raw cashew flour (made in food processor or blender)

      ⅓ C coconut oil

      2-3 Tbsp. raw agave nectar

      ½ C sauerkraut juice (I like Bubbie's)

Add all ingredients to blender and mix until frosting consistency.

Coconut Chocolate Ganache (V,GF)

Thanks for the recipe, Aimee (www.aimeehenrikson.blogspot.com)!

My Coconut Chocolate Ganache is prepared with coconut milk instead of the heavy cream used in traditional recipes. For best results, use the type of chocolate noted here.

      8 oz. good-quality, dairy-free dark chocolate, coarsely chopped

      1 (15 oz.) can coconut milk (regular, not lite variety)

      ⅓ C coconut palm sugar, ground fine in a coffee grinder or blender

      1½ tsp. vanilla extract

Place the dark chocolate in a medium-sized bowl and set aside. In a small saucepan over medium-high heat, heat the coconut milk and sugar until bubbles just begin to appear around the edges and steam rises from the surface. Pour the hot milk/sugar mixture over the chopped chocolate and let stand without stirring for 5 min. After 5 min., stir the mixture until glossy and smooth (this will take about 2 min. of gentle stirring). Add the vanilla and stir gently. Pour over cake or torte.

Yummy Chocolate Frosting (V,GF)

Thanks for the recipe, Aimee (www.aimeehenrikson.blogspot.com)!

½ C coconut oil or ghee (clarified butter, available in health food stores)

2 C powdered coconut sugar (grind in small batches in a coffee grinder)

1 Tbsp. vanilla extract

2 Tbsp. almond milk

⅓ C raw cacao powder (or more)

dash finely ground Celtic sea salt

Whip all ingredients together to create this yummy frosting.

Frozen Treats

Non-Dairy Strawberry Ice Cream (R,V,GF)

Thanks for the recipe, Amy!

> 3½ - 4 C frozen strawberries
> 1-1½ C cold, unsweetened almond milk (preferably homemade)
> *optional*: 1½ - 2 dates or any natural sweetener (if you want it kind of sweet)
> *optional*: 1-2 (or more) small chunks frozen banana, to thicken

Blend until smooth in high-powered blender. Enjoy!

> **Tip:** You can freeze the almond milk in ice cube trays if you want your ice cream to be harder.

Chocolate Shake (R,V,GF)

Thanks for the recipe, Anitka!

> 1½ handfuls spinach
> ½ C water
> 1 banana
> 1 tsp. - 1 Tbsp. bee pollen
> 1 tsp. raw carob or cocoa powder

Put bee pollen in the blender with the water to dissolve a little. Then add the rest of ingredients and mix well. Add more or less water for desired consistency.

Ice Cream Yum (R,V,GF)

Thanks for the recipe, Debbie!

    1 frozen banana

    1 C frozen mixed berries or 1 of your choice

    2-3 C any greens (I like romaine)

    1 tsp. maca powder

    1 Tbsp. psyllium powder

    1 scoop raw protein (Garden of Life)

    optional: 1 Tbsp. raw cocoa

Blend in blender until all ingredients are combined.

Almond Joyful Ice Cream (R,V,GF)

Thanks for the recipe, Desirée Hancock (www.unconventionalkitchen.com)!

This ice cream is so easy to put together and so good.

Main ingredients:

>2 C (1 can, full fat) coconut milk
>3 C rice or almond milk [Use almond milk for R recipe.]
>½ Tbsp. vanilla
>1 tsp. almond extract
>1 generous C agave
>4 Tbsp. cocoa powder
>1 Tbsp. coconut oil

Mix-ins:

>unsweetened coconut
>dark chocolate chips (or you could do semi sweet)
>coconut oil
>almonds (slivered almonds work even better because you don't have to chop them)

In a high blender blend all the main ingredients together. Be careful not to overblend the mixture or the coconut milk will start separating. Process in an ice cream maker according to its directions.

While the ice cream is processing, toast the mix-in coconut and almonds on a cookie sheet in the oven. You can broil them on low or toast them in a 400° oven. Watch carefully! Coconut toasts really fast. When toasted, give the almonds a rough chop (if not using slivered).

In a sauce pan, melt the mix-in chocolate chips and coconut oil together. (I usually melt a generous ½ C chocolate chips with about 1 Tbsp. coconut oil.)

Once the ice cream is thick and almost done, drizzle in the melted chocolate and then stir in the toasted coconut and almonds.

Raw Cinnamon Ice Cream (R,V,GF)

Thanks for the recipe, Desirée Hancock (www.unconventionalkitchen.com)!

    2 C coconut milk
    2 C almond milk
    2-3 tsp. ground cinnamon (to taste)
    1/2-1 C agave (to taste)
    ½ tsp. sea salt

Blend all of the ingredients in a high-powered blender. Transfer the mixture to an ice cream maker and follow its directions. Alternatively, you could freeze the mixture in ice cube trays and when you are craving ice cream, just blend the ice cubes with a little bit of almond milk! If it is not thick enough, add regular ice cubes.

Rawkin Raspberry Ice Cream (R,V,GF)

Thanks for the recipe, Desirée Hancock (www.unconventionalkitchen.com)!

This ice cream is so good with fresh berries, but frozen would work too. I also like to make this ice cream with mixed berries: black berries, raspberries, and strawberries.

    2 C almond milk
    2 C coconut milk
    ½ - 1 C agave (depending on how sweet your berries are)
    3 C raspberries
    1 Tbsp. lemon juice or zest from one lemon
    1½ tsp. vanilla

Blend all of the ingredients except for the raspberries in a high-powered blender. Add the raspberries into the blender and pulse until you have small bits of raspberries. Process in an ice cream maker according to its directions.

Banamon Ice (R,V,GF)

Thanks for the recipe, Elayne!

> 1 young coconut (meat and liquid)*
> 1 handful soaked, pitted dates (raw honey can be used instead of dates)
> 1 tsp. vanilla
> ½ tsp. cinnamon (or to taste)
> 4-5 frozen bananas, chunked
> *optional*: 1 Tbsp. organic, raw cocoa powder or carob

*OK to use frozen coconut meat and pure water if you have no coconut water.

In a high-powered blender, add coconut meat and some of the liquid—just enough to blend the meat. (It doesn't matter if the meat is like jelly or up to ¼" thick. If thicker, it may well retain texture—which tastes good too, but it has a different feel in the mouth.) Also add the dates, vanilla, cinnamon, and optional cocoa, then blend together well. While blender is running, gradually add the banana chunks to the mixture and blend until smooth. Enjoy this yummy soft ice cream immediately!

> *Tip:* If it turns out too runny, give it an hour in the freezer before eating.

Green Pudding Popsicles (R,V,GF)

Thanks for the recipe, Emily!

> ½ fresh pineapple, cubed
> 2 C mango chunks, frozen and partially thawed
> 2 handfuls spinach or collard greens

Put pineapple in blender and blend to make your liquid base—don't add any water! Blend in the greens. Add mango chunks and blend well. Pour into popsicle molds and freeze. You can also serve this just as a pudding by pouring it into serving dishes and eating immediately.

Lemon-Blueberry Frozen Pulse Dessert (R,V,GF)

Thanks for the recipe, Linda "Louise" (www.lindalouise.org)!

A refreshing, tangy, not-too-sweet, antioxidant-rich frozen dessert.

> ½ C liquid coconut oil (I melt coconut oil in dehydrator at 105°)
> ½ Tbsp. sunflower lecithin
> ¾ C fresh lemon juice
> 1 organic lemon, sliced (rind and all, but no seeds)
> ¼ C coconut water from young coconut
> ½ C coconut meat from young coconut
> 2 avocados
> ¾ C raw coconut nectar (Coconut Secrets)
> ½ C blueberries
> ⅛ tsp. sea salt
> *optional*: 2 drops stevia liquid, vanilla flavor

Combine the first two ingredients well and set aside. In a high-powered blender, blend the rest of the ingredients together. Then add the coconut oil/lecithin mixture and blend several minutes until very well incorporated, being careful not to overheat. Blend in two batches if needed. Finished product should be smooth and free of lumps. Pour into glass container with a lid and place in freezer overnight. Scoop and enjoy like ice cream.

Avocado Mexican Ice Cream (R,V,GF)

Thanks for the recipe, Lisette Puerto!

I created this recipe to take the place of the Mexican version with dairy milk.

> 3 young coconuts (meat only; save liquid for other use)
> 1 Tbsp. vanilla bean
> 2 avocados, pitted
> 6 organic dates
> 4 C ice cubes
> *optional*: raw chocolate pieces

Mix all together in the blender and enjoy.

Chocolate "Milkshake" (R,V,GF)

Thanks for the recipe, Marci!

> 3-4 frozen bananas
> 2 C rice milk or water (or a combination of both)
> ½ C raw almonds or cashews
> 1 handful chopped dates *OR* a few whole dates
> 1 Tbsp. cocoa powder [Use raw cocoa powder for R recipe.]
> ¼ tsp. cinnamon
> heavy pinch nutmeg
> ⅛ - ¼ tsp. ginger powder
> 1 tsp. pure vanilla

Blend it all together and enjoy!

> **Tip:** When I don't have frozen bananas, I use fresh and add some ice to make it frozen. Sometimes I add a little extra ice anyway to make it smoother.

Stefanie's Anytime "Ice Cream" (R,V,GF)

Thanks for the recipe, Stephanie!

This "ice cream" is so healthy it can even be eaten for breakfast—or anytime!

> ½ C whole almonds *OR* ¼ C sliced almonds
> 2 C frozen strawberries
> 2 fresh bananas
> 1 splash water, rice milk, almond milk, or coconut milk

Mix almonds, strawberries, and bananas in the blender and mix until smooth. Use the smallest amount of milk/water, just to get it through the blender. Mix it all until it is very creamy. Scoop it into a bowl and enjoy immediately.

Puddings & Custards

Quinoa Pudding (GF)

Thanks for the recipe, Angela!

> 3 C cooked quinoa
>
> 2 C almond milk (blend ¼ C almonds with 2 C water; don't strain)
>
> 1 egg (organic, free range)
>
> 2 tsp. vanilla
>
> ⅓ C coconut palm sugar
>
> 20-30 drops liquid stevia (or to taste)
>
> *optional*: cinnamon, raisins, currants, pecans, maple syrup, cocoa powder (non-alkalized), for toppings

Mix cooked quinoa and 1½ C milk over medium heat until bubbly. Stir about 10 min. until it thickens a bit. Stir in sugar.

Mix egg with remainder ½ C milk and pour into quinoa mixture. Continue mixing until rich and creamy, about 5-10 more min. Add in stevia drops. Take off heat and add vanilla. Serve warm or cold and sprinkled with optional toppings.

Avocado Pudding (R,V,GF)

Thanks for the recipe, Barb!

> 1 Tbsp. raw almond butter
>
> 2 Tbsp. chia gel
>
> ¼ C coconut milk
>
> ½ tsp. vanilla
>
> ½ tsp. stevia powder
>
> ½ avocado, mashed
>
> 2 Tbsp. frozen blueberries
>
> 1 Tbsp. chopped cranberries
>
> *optional*: ⅛ tsp. almond extract

Mix the first six ingredients together, then fold in the berries. Blend until smooth.

Monkey's Favorite Custard (R,V,GF)

Thanks for the recipe, Elizabeth!

> 2 bananas
> 1 handful ice
> ¾ - 1 C water
> 1-2 Tbsp. peanut, almond, or coconut butter *OR* 1 handful raw almonds
> *optional*: 1 Tbsp. raw cacao nibs (if you don't have a Blendtec or other high-powered blender, use cacao powder instead)

I use the Whole Juice setting on my Blendtec blender.

Green Pudding (R,V,GF)

Thanks for the recipe, Emily!

> ½ fresh pineapple, cubed
> 2 C mango chunks, frozen and partially thawed
> 2 handfuls spinach or collard greens

Put pineapple in blender and blend to make your liquid base—don't add any water! Blend in the greens. Add mango chunks and blend well. Pour into serving dishes and eating immediately.

Chocolate Pudding (R,V,GF)

Thanks for the recipe, Jami!

> 3 avocados
> ¼ C + 3 Tbsp. raw agave
> ¼ C + 2 Tbsp. raw cocoa
> 3 Tbsp. raw almond butter
> 1 tsp. fresh lemon juice
> pinch cinnamon
> pinch nutmeg or cardamom
> ½ tsp. extract of choice (vanilla, mint, etc.)

Blend all ingredients in food processor until pudding-like! So good! I've even ad-libbed a dab of coconut oil, just because! It's a fatty treat and very decadent, so a little goes a long way! Yummy!

Millet Pudding (GF)

Thanks for the recipe, Leena!

This is good either hot or cold and is a fun alternative to rice pudding.

> ¾ C millet
> 3 C coconut milk
> ½ C raw honey
> 1 C coconut flakes
> 1 tsp. salt
> 1 tsp. honey

Preheat oven to 300°. Mix all the ingredients together. Place in an oiled casserole dish and bake for 1-1½ hr. Eat hot/warm or chill to eat cold. *Makes ~ 5 1-cup servings*. [See Photos section.]

Raw Chocolate Mousse (R,V,GF)

Thanks for the recipe, Michael and RaeVern!

> 1 whole young coconut
> 1 C organic raw cashews (unsoaked)
> 1 Tbsp. raw cacao powder (Sunfood Nutrition)
> 2 Tbsp. raw agave nectar
> ½ vanilla bean *OR* 1 tsp. vanilla extract
> dash Himalayan or other sea salt
> 6-8 ice cubes (crushed is ideal)

Cut vanilla bean half and remove ends of stem, add cashews, cacao powder, agave, and sea salt. Pulse very briefly in blender, making sure everything is mixed. Poke the coconut and drain the water into blender. Open the coconut, scrape out the coconut meat, and put in the blender and blend all on high speed until smooth. Add ice and blend again until frozen and creamy. Pour into serving bowls and refrigerator for 2 hr. or until stiff.

Plain Chia Pudding (R,V,GF)

Thanks for the recipe, Rebecca!

> 1 C chia seeds
> 3 C nut milk (could also use coconut or hemp milk)
> 3-5 Tbsp. raw agave nectar
> pinch sea salt
> *optional*: 1 tsp. vanilla extract
> *optional*: ¼ tsp. cinnamon

Place the chia seeds, milk, agave, and salt in a bowl along with optional vanilla and/or cinnamon and stir well so there are no clumps and all the chia seeds are coated in milk. Let this sit at room temperature for 20-30 min. before eating—or cover and refrigerate overnight. This pudding will keep well in the refrigerator for days.

For a chocolate version (my favorite), omit the cinnamon and replace it with 1 Tbsp. cocoa powder. [See Photos section.]

Avocado Pudding Too (R,V,GF)

Thanks for the recipe, Sharla!

> 1 avocado
> 1 Tbsp. cocoa [Use raw cocoa for R recipe.]
> ¼ tsp. green Stevia
> pinch sea salt
> splash vanilla extract

Blend or process all ingredients. We usually triple the recipe and eat it straight from the processor!

Carob-Avocado Pudding (V,GF)

Thanks for the recipe, Sharla!

> 1 avocado
> ⅛ C carob
> ⅛ C real maple syrup
> sea salt, to taste

Blend or process all ingredients. Another yummy recipe that we usually triple and eat straight from the processor!

Other Desserts

Dried Fig Bliss (R,V,GF)

Thanks for the recipe, Alex!

>4 large pears, peeled and seeded
>3.5 oz. tepid water
>2 pinches tumeric
>pinch salt
>250 g. dried figs
>1 apple, peeled and cored
>½ C unsweetened apple juice (fresh, if possible)
>½ tsp. cardamon
>¼ tsp. cinnamon
>juice of ½ lemon (or to taste)

Cut pears into long slices, cover them with tepid water, add turmeric and salt, and let them marinate for a while.

Put apple juice, apples, figs, cinnamon, and cardamon in a blender and blend well until smooth. Add lemon juice and blend briefly again to incorporate; adjust for taste if needed.

Put the purée on serving plates. Drain the pears and arrange some slices like a fan over the purée on each plate. *Makes 4 servings.*

Sweet Butternut Squash Dessert (V,GF)

Thanks for the recipe, Juanique!

If you don't tell them, your kids will never know that this yummy dessert is a vegetable!

> 1 medium- to large-sized organic butternut squash
> ½ C organic raisins
> ½ C chopped organic walnuts
> ½ Tbsp. organic cinnamon
> 1 Tbsp. organic coconut butter/oil
> organic raw agave

Preheat oven to 350°. Cut squash in half, remove seeds, and bake face down on a flat sheet for about 45 min. to 1 hr. Scrape the squash into a bowl (preferably glass) and mix it until its mushy. Add the rest of the ingredients, to taste, and mix well.

Dried Fruit Compote (V,GF)

Thanks for the recipe, Mira Dessy (www.grainsandmore.blogspot.com)!

> 1 C dried prunes
> 1 C dried apricots
> 1 C raisins (I prefer Thompson's)
> unsweetened apple juice, enough to cover fruit (fresh, if possible)
> zest of ½ orange
> ¼ C Sucanat or coconut palm sugar
> 1 cinnamon stick
> 2 cloves
> ¼ tsp. fresh nutmeg

Put fruit and apple juice into a sauce pan, bring to a boil, cover, and reduce to a simmer. Add all other ingredients and simmer another 20-30 min., stirring occasionally (compote will thicken as fruit softens). Remove zest, cinnamon, and cloves, then set aside to cool completely before serving. *Makes 4 servings.*

> **Tip:** Apricots and Thompson raisins are easy to find in most grocery stores without preservatives (usually marked either "organic" or "unsulfured").Trader Joe's and Earthbound Farms both have preservative-free dried plums; they can also be ordered online from NutsOnline.com and Amazon.com.

Banana Festive (R,V,GF)

Thanks for the recipe, Myria!

> 10-12 bananas
> ½ C cashews
> 4 dates, pitted
> 2 prunes, pitted
> juice of 1 apple

Blend the cashews in a blender until they become powder, then empty into a bowl.

Whisk well the apple juice with the dates and prunes. Then add the bananas and blend again very well. Pour the contents over the cashews powder and stir with a spoon to become a cream and serve.

Healthy "Sundae" (GF)

Thanks for the recipe, Paula!

> ½ C low-fat plain yogurt
> 1 Tbsp. shredded sweetened coconut
> 4-5 fresh strawberries
> ½ tsp. chopped almonds

Mix yogurt and coconut, then top with strawberries and almonds. This tastes a lot like a strawberry Sunday, only better! [See Photos section.]